BECOMING THE ULTIMATE IT

Table of Contents

1

WHAT YOU
SHOULD KNOW

Be Who And What You Want.
You Are About To Change Your Life. This Is It.

This book was written with the thought to elevate, inspire and change you. Everything you believe about yourself that is limiting, self-deprecating and critical we ask you to let it go. We want you to drop your memory of who you believed you were and use this book to formulate a much better version of yourself and the IT Girl that we know that you will be. This book was created for you to start seeing yourself as an IT Girl. We want you to read this book, take notes in a separate journal and read this book again. Remember to apply what you read. You will see that we start with addressing your inner thoughts and views of yourself and work our way to discussing style, outward appearance and overall environment as an IT Girl.

We wrote this book already assuming you are an IT Girl. We talk to you as an IT Girl even though we know this is a guide to becoming the best IT Girl you want to be. We talk to you like a friend. This is a conversation from us IT Girls to you. We do use our own verbiage for playfulness and well because we can. This book is written exactly how we talk. So forget everything you heard about what an IT Girl is and you'll learn how you can be and will be an IT Girl yourself.

IT Girl Luxury was founded by Tatiana Jerome who loves everything about fashion but also knows the importance of working from the inside out. What started as just playing around with styles has now become a way to make women of all ages live their authentic selves, enjoy their femininity, and put themselves on a pedestal. Ditch the old way of living with the limitations of who you think you have to be and start getting what you want, operating in your space of authenticity, and being loved through it all. Once you accept yourself as that IT Girl, everyone around you will see and love you as that girl as well. This book is for you. IT Girl Luxury is now a community and we want you to know you are now part of the community of IT Girls that now live their lives on their terms. If you can't believe that now, you will believe that once you are done reading this book. We repeat a lot of things because we want them embedded in you and how important it is. You'll see as you continue reading. Now unto the next pages of the definition of an IT Girl. Don't skip this section. You'll need it to understand where you fit in in the world of IT Girls. All right, turn the page.

2

THE DEFINITION

What Is An IT Girl?

So when you look up the definition of an IT Girl, you typically run into the definition of a young attractive female or a young woman who has achieved celebrity status because of her socialite lifestyle and/or has sex appeal and a personality that is especially engaging. And that is it. It stops there. Well we like to say ummmmm nooooooo! There is so much more to an IT Girl that we had to write this guide and truly redefine what an IT Girl is. While we use the term IT Girl, it is not exclusive to just young girls. IT Girls to us are women of all ages. Whether you are in your teens, twenties, thirties, forties, fifties and sixties... you can be an IT Girl (why wouldn't you want to be that amazing IT Girl in your sixties?). Youth is all in how you feel and carry yourself. You've probably seen some women in their forties look and act more youthful than some women in their twenties.

Being an IT Girl is more than just being physically attractive. An IT Girl doesn't just have sex appeal, she is confident. She is alluring. She is positive. She takes care of herself inside and out. She is stylish. She is comfortable in her own femininity. She is mysterious. She is irresistible. She makes everything seem so effortless. She has a way of drawing you in and making you feel good about the decisions you make as well as the decisions she may want you to make. She is a leader. She is the trend. She is the muse. She is the one that others seek approval from. She is an inspiration. She makes others feel good around her. She helps others. She has authority. She is unshakeable. She is an IT Girl because she knows who she is. This is our definition of an IT Girl. This is who we are talking about. This is who we are and this is who we hope we can inspire you to be. Why? Simply because it's a wonderful life. Being an IT Girl isn't for everyone because it requires an individual to make a decision to implement changes within one's own life. It requires you to ask yourself if you are finally ready to work on you. This means the inner and outer work you have either been neglecting or simply didn't believe you needed to do.

But let us quickly tell you what being an IT Girl doesn't mean. You can't simply be an IT Girl because you have money, or because you come from a certain background or you have certain outwardly things you believe others do not have. This isn't about material possessions. You may be able to buy your way for a fake IT Girl status for a while but it won't last forever because once a true IT Girl is around, everyone will be able to see and recognize her. So it's not about having an education, way of dressing or being around celebrities. You can have a small circle and be the IT Girl of your circle, community, job and so on or be the biggest celebrity or socialite if that is what you desire. But we want you to know that you can be an IT Girl. It's all in the way you view yourself and that starts with being the main character of your life.

3

BEING THE MAIN CHARACTER OF YOUR OWN LIFE

The definition of a main character: The most important character of the story. The focus of any story.

Your life. Your story. How do you choose to tell it? Have you started romanticizing your life? Are you seeing things as everything working out for you instead of against you? Being the main character in your own life means that you are lifting yourself up in all ways of thought and acts. This doesn't mean being self-centered or just rude to others. This means viewing yourself as the one that things works out for. Viewing yourself as the deserving one. This is a mindful state of just being. Being a main character also is in knowing that everyone around you is a supporting character in your story of life. You must start to realize that you are the everyday main character and not a side kick. You are not playing the guest starring role. You are not an audience member and not a bystander. You as a main character must start showing up for you and viewing yourself as having the most important role. Regardless of what you call flaws or setbacks, you are the main character which means stop putting others on a pedestal. No one should be on a pedestal above you. Not a celebrity, not a crush, not someone you admire....no one should be placed on a pedestal. If you currently have someone one a high pedestal above you, take them off that pedestal right now. There is no reason why anyone but you should be seen or deemed as better than you regardless of what you think you know about them or what the world is trying to sell you about them. This is your life and this is about you. When you start to romanticize your life, you start upgrading even the simplest things of what you do. From things like making your bed, taking a walk and any little act that makes up your everyday routine to making it better and favorable for you. This would be called romanticizing your life. Falling in love with the details. The idea of romanticizing your life is to make the biggest and smallest things appear better because of the details you give to it. It's the experience of the most minute tasks that we make seem wonderful. It's in how you layout your breakfast or sip on your tea. These details truly matter because they are all done for you. In the beginning your thoughts might be who am I doing this for, this is time consuming, why am I doing this... etc. You may even find that you may think that this is absolutely not necessary for you, but we're saying it is. If you were to see another IT Girl and see the details that are done for her and her life then you would see that these things may be parts of being an IT Girl that you admire and that is because she is the main character and every detail is for her attention. When you ask yourself why you are doing this and who are you doing this for ...the answer should be for you. You again. You being the main character and now it is time to act like it. This is about you. This is all for you. Things can only change because of you. Everything you think and feel and believe will reflect within your life because of you. Again this all revolves around you. You set the rules. You create the boundaries. You take accountability. You decided what stays and what goes. You choose how you will show up. You have the choice to elevate. Whatever circumstances you created, you can solve. You get to choose what you accept. Once you accept that you are the main character, you will no longer play victim to anything. You will no longer see yourself as a victim, act as a victim and make decisions as a victim. You will get into main character behavior and start moving the right pieces in your life as an IT Girl. Your power as an IT Girl will start to show itself from inside out and we truly know it all starts when you currently know how you perceive yourself.

4

SELF-PERCEPTION

It's time to take inventory. Take the time to think about how you view yourself on a day-to-day bases. Do you believe that everything works out in your favor? Do you expect things to go badly and say things like of course that would happen to me? Do you feel bad because of past mistakes or your current situation and do not see a way to get out of it? Are your decisions based on what others may think about you or react? How do you want to start viewing yourself? Take a piece of paper or a journal and start writing down the woman you want to become. As we said earlier, it doesn't matter your age, you can decide to change and even be more fabulous than you are right now. How do you want to feel every day? What changes do you see yourself implementing? These changes could be inner changes, outward changes, or both. We always encourage inner change before anything to be able to effectively do outward changes. Don't limit yourself. Once you know what changes you want and how you want to start living, you'll want to ask yourself a series of questions. Why do you want these changes and who are these changes for? Will these changes make you feel better about yourself? Are these changes being done for you and not for anyone else? It's okay if others benefit from your change but they must first be done for you and your motivation for these changes should be for how you want to see yourself and how you want to elevate. When you take the time to write down how you view yourself you are also taking the time to understand how you got to where you are today. If you currently do not view yourself as a powerful main character in your own story, it is okay. All of that is now going to change. Once you write down how you want to start viewing yourself, it's now time to write down how you want to start talking to yourself. Your thoughts, and your inner conversations all matter. What are you saying to yourself? What do you constantly keep affirming daily? You probably do not even realize it, but every day with every thought you are constantly affirming. You are constantly telling yourself how great something is or isn't. What you can and cannot do and so on. When you say 'I am tired' so many times you are constantly affirming that you are just that....tired. Again so what are you saying to yourself? It's probably time for you to have a new conversation with yourself about the type of IT Girl you are becoming. What do you want to tell yourself every morning, every night, and during the day? What will you start telling yourself to start believing? What beliefs do you want/need to let go of to feel like you and be free? Well, let's start with you telling yourself that you are strongly loved. That you are an IT Girl. Everything that you want unfolds and happens for you so effortlessly and instantly. These are affirmations. Affirmations are positive statements that you make towards yourself that you repeat to yourself constantly throughout the day. Eventually, you'll start to believe your affirmations and become who you say you are. Here are some examples of some positive IT Girl affirmations you can use for yourself:

- I Always Get What I Want.
- Everything Always Works Out For Me Because I Said So.
- I Always Have Positive Thoughts.
- I Am The Woman Who Has It All.
- I Am Always Spoiled By Others.
- I Exude Sex Appeal.
- I Am Always The Priority.
- I Am Gorgeous.
- My Body Is Perfection.
- I Am Healthy.
- I Am Wealthy.
- I Am Always Loved, Cherished And Chosen.
- I Am Intelligent.
- I Am The Best Version Of Myself Right Now.
- I Am Confident.
- All Men Are Naturally Attracted To Me And I Am Naturally Every Guys Dream Woman.
- I Am Desired. I Am Pursued.
- I Accepted.

- I Appreciate Myself.
- I Am Always Safe To Be Myself.
- I Am Always Catered To.
- I Am Loved.
- I Am So Beautiful.
- I Am An IT Girl.
- I Am Royalty.
- I Get Better Looking Every Day.

These are just some of the affirmations you can use for yourself depending on what you want to work on and what you want to believe about you. You can use these affirmations or create your own affirmations that would feel and sound natural to you. Now we know you might be thinking, well I just don't believe my affirmations. My mind is laughing at me telling me these aren't true and even giving me examples of moments that contradict what I am saying. And we say your mind is doing what it is supposed to be doing. It is trying to say 'are we sure about this new routine?' You haven't said these things about yourself before. Do we as a whole really believe this? Your response to your mind should be authoritative. You would tell it that this is the new truth about us (you) , and that it will need to accept this new truth whether it likes it or not. You will have to keep repeating this to yourself. Anytime you hear your mind tell you the opposite of what you are trying to affirm, this is where you say to it very loudly NO and flip your thoughts. This takes work. This is just the beginning of the work that you must do for your main character energy to start showing out and shining. Flip your negative thoughts. Do not suppress them. Do not fight against them. Just correct it like you are correcting a child with your inner conversation and tell it this is what we will be thinking every day, all day long till you get it. Train your mind to focus on your better you. After creating your affirmation routine that we recommend that you say to yourself every morning, night and throughout the day; you will start to see yourself becoming the person you want to be. This is how you build yourself up to be the IT Girl you know you are. It starts from within. This is a lifestyle and with this daily work, you'll start to notice an increase in your confidence. We will move forward in this book and affirm from this point out that you are an IT Girl.

5

BUILDING
SELF-CONFIDENCE

Chin Up Princess Or The Crown Slips

Now that we have a foundation for our self-perception and our daily self-talk and affirmational thoughts, it's time for you as an IT Girl to realize that your self-confidence in yourself must be built. The good news is that through affirmations and just affirming that you are confident, you are already on the path to building your self-confidence. What does the path to confidence look like? Well, that first starts with self-talk and perception. Let's address some hard-hitting truths that come with the confidence you need as an IT Girl. IT Girls do the following:

- Work On Themselves
- Work Through Past Mistakes
- Thinks About Her Possibilities
- Sets Goals
- Spends Time Creating And Practicing Her Physical Routine To Stay Active
- Learns And Understands Herself
- Works Through Any Insecurities She May Have
- Cutting Back On Negative And Toxic Energy
- Spends Time With Other Confident Women
- She Knows When To Say No And How To Say It

Work On Themselves

This is exactly what you are doing now. Take the first step to decide what you want to work on. Then decide to dedicate a portion of your day (every day) to work towards that. By putting the focus on your goals and by truly working on them, you will see that your daily commitment to the work that you put in will start to show and no longer feel like work. It will be just part of what you do.

Work Through Past Mistakes

When you want to move forward, there will be times when you'll want to look back. Why? Well, it could be because you feel yourself progressing and you have mixed emotions about leaving some things behind, or it could also be that you truly don't recognize yourself with or without certain elements of your past. The new version of you is shedding your past. But as an IT Girl, it's important to work through past mistakes so they no longer hinder you. By choosing to work on forgiving yourself and your past mistakes, it can help you to make better decisions in your present and future. When you acknowledge your past mistakes you take the power away from it and it can no longer be used against you. Taking the time to truly work through something that keeps replaying in your head or triggers you, not only heals you but graduates you to the IT Girl who realizes that she is not her mistakes and that she can rise from anything.

Thinks About Her Possibilities

IT Girls live in their possibilities because they know that they will become a reality. We live in love, our accomplishments, helping others and so much more. Limitations have been removed from any sentence and thought and it is no longer a matter of if but when. By becoming the IT Girl we know you are, you will start to learn how to command what you want into your life. You know everything is possible for you. You are not your old thoughts and other people's limitations of themselves. When everyone else is talking about living in this 'reality world,' your reality world looks so much different because it conforms to you simply because you are the main character. It's an anything is possible type of world for you.

Set Goals

Whether personal or professional, there are always goals to be set and accomplishments ready to be achieved. Life doesn't just happen to you as an IT Girl. It happens because of you. It happens because you have steered your focus to a goal. When goals are not set, you have made a decision to also allow anything to happen because of you. You are what you believe you can and cannot do. Setting goals for yourself and creating steps to achieve those goals helps to build the confidence that every IT Girl carries within herself. With some goals, you may face some challenges, but it is by overcoming them that helps you to build the trust and faith within yourself to accomplish so much more.

Spends Time Creating And
Practicing Her Physical Routine To Stay Active

If you do not have one already, we recommend creating a thirty-minute physical routine that you can do each day or every other day to stay active to help grow your confidence in yourself and your body. No more talking about your body or the lack of appreciation you have for your body. Whether it is a thirty-minute walk, swim, yoga session or just spending time at the gym; creating an active physical routine for yourself will help you to reduce stress, and create a positive self-image of yourself while creating a sense of accomplishment each time you do it. You'll also start to feel confident in whatever else you set out to achieve in your life. By staying active you are also practicing self-love.

Learns And Understands Herself

IT Girls gain confidence by taking the time to learn and understand themselves. This means knowing what we like and what we do not like, knowing who we are, how we have evolved, our current strengths and weakness as well as what makes us react. We always have time for ourselves. This is the time to figure out what you love, what are you passionate about, and what types of people you want around you. Understanding yourself means being able to express grace in the areas that you fall short. When you can learn about yourself, you can then easily make the necessary changes to get you to the most higher level of operating as an IT Girl.

Dealing With Insecurities

We do not like to say that everyone has an insecurity because well we just do not know and do not believe that. We do believe that some of us once had an insecurity and now have evolved from it to where we no longer consider that an insecurity. There is nothing wrong with knowing and/or learning about your insecurities and where they come from. But the real question is how do you deal with it every day to your advantage? How do you now make your insecurities work for you? For example, if your awkwardness makes you awkward then embrace your awkwardness.

The best way to overcome your insecurities is to confront your feelings and affirm your value. You are not less than because of your insecurities. Once you know this and start affirming your value, you start to make your insecurities look small. What do we mean by this? We mean not allowing it to seem like this big monster holding you back. We know a lot of insecurities fall in the following areas...social insecurity, body image, relationship, basic needs and not being good enough because of what you may feel you don't have. To grow in your self-confidence you must inhabit a growth mindset. Through this mindset, you will learn you are not a failure because of your insecurities, but by acknowledging them and working through your feelings you will be able to shift your perspective and start to watch what you say to yourself and check that if what you are saying to yourself is a hard concrete fact or more a story you are telling yourself. By doing this your inner conversation starts to change and you start to mold yourself into the IT Girl who doesn't allow this now former insecurity to have that kind of power. You are no longer to be a slave to the insecurity that tries to remind you of a former story you told yourself which causes you to feel as if you must be perfect. You can truly be yourself and no longer allow the insecurity to tell you how to behave that is keeping you from really receiving the IT Girl treatment. This in turn helps you to build your self-confidence.

Cutting Back On Negative And Toxic Energy

We don't have time for the drama! We do not put out energy towards people who do not believe in us and what we are doing. IT Girls clean up their space inside and out. We have been focusing a lot on first our inner beliefs and thoughts but we are also aware of the spaces we place ourselves in, whom we hang around, and the conversations we entertain. If you have negative people around you, stop dealing with them immediately. Just stop. If what you want to see for yourself is more important than the negativity that you are comfortable with then you will make this change. It is time to let go of not only negative thoughts that hinder confidence but the negative people around you that support your negative thoughts and help build new negative thoughts. If you live with negative people or have to deal with negativity in your workplace or any other area of your life, it's time for you to demand your space back. You do so by simply switching what you focus on. No more agreeing for the sake of agreeing. No more disagreeing for the sake of having them see things your way. No more. You are changing you and so everything around you will have to change. This means attitude. This means beliefs, and this also means negative talk. This means removing yourself from environments that do not support the woman you say you want to be. Removing yourself from these things may feel like they are not easy to do at first (especially when it has consumed almost every area of your life), but when you decide that the toxic talk and toxic actions will no longer drive you to move the way you do then you will start to gain self-confidence in who you are. You will start to see that no one can make you do or be anything. When you start to take accountability for some negative thoughts and toxic behaviors you may have exhibited, you will have to decide what you will stop doing. The changes within your environment, as well as the people around you, will reflect how you view yourself. IT Girls are not jealous nor do we entertain jealous behavior. We relax and know that we are IT. We move and operate always knowing that we are IT and are more effective in the most positive of environments to be and do what we want to do. If you are in a toxic environment, now is the time to create your exit strategy. This means knowing how you will leave, planning your exit, knowing what you will be leaving behind, considering what are you gaining, knowing where you are going, and having a plan on how you will move forward to protect your peace and how will you stop yourself from going back and attracting toxic environments in your space. But while you are in the current toxic environment you must still be able to operate and grow. This means reflecting before you act and every day providing yourself with the tools to keep yourself focused on you.

You may be wondering what are some signs of a toxic person and if can you change them. There are some people that we love so much but wish they saw and knew better. We often wished they would stop being negative and stop putting others and themselves down. Some of these individuals are considered toxic people due to the following traits:

- They Are Easily Jealous
- They Constantly Act As A Victim
- They Are Constantly Looking For Pity And Attention
- They Give Backhanded Compliments
- They Love To Guilt Trip You
- They Like To Bully Others

There is no real way to change toxic and/or negative people. The only thing you can do is establish boundaries and not allow them to pull you into the deliberate drama that they create nor take what they say personally. Be sure to create and surround yourself with healthy relationships. Do not look to these people for support or validation in any form as it will never be enough. Do not let individuals who you consider negative be the reason to get you out of character. This is where you will learn to choose your battles wisely. As you stay protective of your space and set up boundaries for yourself, you create opportunities for new healthy relationships to show up around you and support your authentic self. Creating this protective space will help you to build your self-confidence in doing what is right for you.

Spends Time With Other Confident Women

To build your self-confidence, the best way to do that is to spend time with other positive confident women. These women could be within your family, new friends, old friends, women you meet who are doing things you want to do, etc. Confident women are women who speak positively of each other always, speak about opportunities, create opportunities, stays true to herself, knows how to be a friend, as well as motivates and inspires you. She has a purpose and embraces her purpose while showing you a new perspective on life. When you spend time with other confident women you start to become more confident in who you are and how you handle certain situations within your life. The secret you probably already figured out is that the MOST confident women are IT Girls.

She Knows When To Say No And How To Say It

One of the main things every self-confident woman knows how to say is no. She knows that people pleasing is exhausting and honoring what feels right to her by saying no when she feels fit is the right thing to do for her. IT Girls know they are not able to be their best for anyone if they are not at peace with themselves. When something that is being asked of you may compromise your morals and values, you can stand up for yourself simply by saying no. This makes you stronger and grows confidence in your abilities to honor yourself. You do not compromise who you are to make sure you are pleasing others. IT Girls do not just say no when necessary but also know how to say no without being rude or feeling guilty. If it is hard for you to say no start off by first rehearsing with yourself in the mirror saying no and not giving an explanation. By being able to communicate your desire to say no you will learn to be your authentic self. By communicating your thoughts with self-confidence you can stand firm in who you are. While many times we want to say no but do not say it because we don't want to hurt someone's feelings, we want to be accepted and/or liked, or we don't know how to stand up for ourselves; we know that by practicing and exercising your right to say no you will start to see yourself experiencing less stress, less wasted energy and fewer people taking advantage of your kindness.

The Difference Between Confidence And Self-Confidence

While these two words are at times used interchangeably there is a slight difference between the two and we believe you should know it. The word confidence is understood to mean to have 'confidence in one's ability and judgment or someone else's ability, judgment, or attributes. The word self-confidence means specifically confidence in yourself or oneself. Self-confidence is directly related to having the inner strength to overcome obstacles as well as the belief in yourself to learn something and over time acquire the confidence to practice and be it.

So when you are working on your self-confidence, you are in essence doing the daily work needed to build inner confidence to deal with anything that may come your way with a sense of knowing that you as an IT Girl can do whatever you want to do effortlessly.

Confidence Or Cocky

Now there is a fine line between being self-confident and just being cocky. The line may be thick for some but thin for many as cocky individuals do have confidence in themselves but also carry an air of arrogance. This arrogance can come from things that an individual may have obtained such as good looks, money, or other external attributes that can easily be removed. An individual who is cocky often sees themselves as superior to others and hardly ever apologizes for their mistakes. These individuals often become cocky when they achieve certain statuses to hide from their insecurities. They put others down so they can feel superior. True IT Girls are not cocky. You should not be cocky if you are doing the inner work needed to deal with insecurities and live in a positive space. We do not put others down. A real IT Girl inspires others and always operates in her authentic self.

It's more than okay to speak highly of yourself even when others are speaking negatively about themselves. You are not trying to fit in or make others feel comfortable with their degrading self-talk. But it is not okay to make others feel bad, bullied, or less than because of what you feel that you are or have. Speaking highly of yourself does not make you cocky because you have self-confidence in yourself despite what others would want you to believe because of their insecurities.

If you find yourself building a false sense of self-confidence based on what you have, you will eventually be brought to a place where what you thought was your foundation will get shaken and disturbed and self-destruction may likely occur because the work wasn't done to build the right foundation. Stay away from cocky individuals and be sure to never build your image on a false sense of who you are through external things you may have obtained that can easily be taken away. Choose real self-confidence over cockiness any day.

In The Process Of Doing The Daily Work To Build Your Self-Confidence, The Thought Of Self-Love Must Come Into Play

Self-love has so many definitions and has taken on so many forms in terms of personal meaning. According to Merriam-Webster, self-love is defined as an appreciation of one's own worth or virtue and proper regard for and attention to one's happiness and well-being. We like to expand that definition by adding that self-love is the full acceptance of yourself through love, kindness, and respect while being able to nurture your wellbeing. Self-love truly is the ability to take care of your own needs and not sacrifice your well-being to please others. Even when you feel like you messed up in some area of your life, you should not practice self-hatred. Self-love encompasses your thoughts and feelings about yourself and how it is reflected in every aspect of your life.

Here are some effective ways to start practicing self-love:

- Meditate Each Day
- Take Some Time To Enjoy Nature Each Day And Be In The Sun. Even If It Is For A Ten Minute Walk
- Allow Yourself Fifteen Minutes Each Day To Sit In Silence
- Look In The Mirror Each Day And Give Yourself A Compliment
- Write A Love Letter To Yourself
- Start Eating Better
- Pamper Yourself Daily
- Declutter Your Life
- Establish Your Own Self-Love Love Language
- If Needed, Seek A Therapist

IT Girls lock in towards self-love and when we say lock-in we mean to make it a natural habit to practice activities that makes us feel good and always stay connected to who we are. In a world filled with things and limiting beliefs created to separate you from your authentic self, self-love is truly a necessity and no longer a luxury.

When you spend more time practicing self-love, you have no time to harp on what you would consider to be your flaws, but instead, you would be developing in areas that would make you happy. You would start to practice gratitude and fall in love with the person you are choosing to evolve to. You would start to see rapid changes in your life in the ways that other people would respond to you and in the way you choose to now live your life. This time is for you. Take that time for it to be about you. Don't just take the lessons from this book and not apply them. Some of our exercises you may have already applied and some you probably haven't heard of; but to truly be the IT Girl that draws attention, our exercises should be practiced consistently to notice the difference.

This is about taking care of you. Doing the inner work required to effortlessly be the IT Girl you envisioned yourself being. So much of this inner work is a major part of the essence of an IT Girl. It's easy to talk fashion, style, money and so much more and we will in the next few chapters but the part that is easily neglected is the inner work that we have mentioned that includes self-confidence building, being comfortable in your skin, self-love and what we will soon be talking about... the emotional, mental and physical well-being needed. That's why when you see an IT Girl she is always an IT Girl because she continues to work on herself and realizes this is her life.

6

TAKING CONTROL OF YOUR EMOTIONAL, PHYSICAL AND SPIRITUAL WELL-BEING

What does the question 'how are you doing?' mean to you? How do you respond to it? Does your answer only reflect on your physical status at that moment? Our well-being involves our body, soul, and spirit. It involves our emotional, physical, and spiritual well-being. For overall fitness, learn to take care of all three. Each aspect of your well-being can affect the other. Therefore, you need to learn to balance them all. When there is no balance between them or when any of them is being neglected, you are affected in different ways. Taking control of your emotional, physical, and spiritual well-being is essential for a healthy lifestyle.

Emotional Well-Being

Your emotional well-being is all about the way you can handle different emotional situations. It is how you can adjust to situations. Your emotional well-being should be taken care of because it is very important and significantly affects not just your overall well-being, but your relationships with others. Good emotional well-being is built on doggedness. IT Girls can exude positivity because our emotional well-being is in a very healthy state. Emotionally healthy people can handle unfavorable conditions better than people who can't control their emotions.

Emotional well-being is important because it helps you face life challenges and enables you to cope even in difficult situations. When you are not emotionally healthy, your mood says it all. You could be cranky, or depressed, or you could have anxiety issues. Maintaining your emotional well-being as IT Girls is all about knowing how to be in control of your emotions and staying resilient at it. Emotionally healthy people have coping mechanisms that help them stay positive, even in negative situations.

Here Are Everyday Tips To Practice:

- ALWAYS HAVING A ROUTINE: Having a routine puts your emotional well-being in check. When you plan your day, you seem to have a balance between your work and the life you live. That way, there is time to also pay attention to your emotional wellbeing.

- PHYSICAL ACTIVITY: Engaging in physical activities can be very refreshing. Activities like workout sessions, dancing, taking long walks, clean-up exercises, or something as simple as rearranging your room, help you be in control of your emotional wellbeing.

- SLEEP: The importance of sleep is underrated. When you have enough sleep, your mood is better and your body feels refreshed too.

- BEING SELF-AWARE: When you are conscious of your attitudes, habits, and characters, you can easily tell when something has gone wrong with you.

- DON'T BE TOO HARD ON YOURSELF: It's okay not to have achieved that goal. It's okay to take things slowly. When you are at peace with yourself, it's easy for you to be at peace with others, too.

- BE KIND: Learn to let go sometimes. Forgive, be kind to people, help people, and connect with them.

- POSITIVITY: Staying positive no matter the situation prevents you from worrying about a lot of things.

Physical Well-Being

Our physical well-being is how we take care of our bodies in general. It involves taking good care of our bodies to improve our quality of life. It is the fuel that drives our bodily functions. The incorporation of healthy lifestyle practices in your daily lives promotes good physical health. Physical well-being is closely related to other well-being. Neglecting your physical well-being can cause chronic stress, poor mental health, fatigue, anxiety, insomnia, and other health-related problems. Therefore, it is important to maintain your physical well-being in the following ways:

- EAT HEALTHILY: Eating healthily is a way of taking care of our bodies. Always take enough water daily to aid the metabolic processes in your body and to prevent dehydration. Do not eat irregularly rather have regular meal patterns. Take more fruits and vegetables too.

- EXERCISES: Engaging in healthy activities such as exercises, help to keep you active and mentally alert. You can also take long walks which are soothing ways to feel the rush of the wind.

- GOING FOR REGULAR HEALTH CHECKUPS: You might think you are all right until you pay a visit to the doctor. Going for checkups regularly is vital for maintaining our physical well-being.

Spiritual Well-Being

Sometimes, when we think of spiritual well-being, we only attribute it to religion. Spiritual well-being explains our connection to a supreme being. It is how deeply connected we are to something higher than us and finding meaning and purpose through our values and beliefs. It involves not only our relationship with a higher being, but it also includes our relationship with ourselves and other people.

Our spiritual well-being is very important. It explains our quest for a deeper meaning in life. We can connect with a higher being and other people, too. When you are spiritually healthy, you can balance major aspects of your life, and you understand your values and live your life in alignment with your beliefs and values.

Here Are Ways To Maintain Your Spiritual Well-Being:

- LOVING YOURSELF: You can't be at your best if you don't take care of yourself. You can only love others with ease when you've learned to love yourself. Caring for yourself helps you to care for others, too. Daily meditation, yoga, taking walks, and journaling are only a few ways of maintaining your spiritual well-being. The other methods of self-care for emotional well-being can also improve our spiritual well-being.

- CONNECTING WITH PEOPLE: You can do this by joining spiritual activities and communities, and engaging in group activities. Teamwork, group activities, and family discussion times can boost your spiritual health. Taking part in shared activities helps us meet people of like minds and this builds our relationships with others too.

- BEING KIND: Appreciating others, and random acts of kindness are all ways to stay socially healthy. It could be by complimenting them with kind words like, 'Hey, I love your outfit', 'your smile is lovely', 'you're children are beautiful', and 'your home is lovely'. Now don't go complimenting people about things that aren't true. You could end up hurting them instead of making them happy. Be genuinely kind to people.

- PRAYER: Spending time with the higher being that you revere, through prayer, is a way to maintain your spiritual wellbeing. This keeps you connected with your supreme being.

- READING SPIRITUAL BOOKS

- CONNECTING WITH NATURE

- FORGIVE: Learn to forgive not just yourself but the people around you. It helps you to be at peace with both yourself and everything around you.

How To Handle Unfavorable Situations

Unfavorable situations can affect your well-being if you are not in control of yourself. Your mode of reacting to situations can be grossly affected if you cannot handle such situations with your well-being in a stable condition. To be in control of your emotional, physical, and spiritual well-being when faced with an unfavorable situation, try the following steps below:

- TAKE A DEEP BREATH: This has a calming effect on your brain.

- QUESTION YOUR THOUGHTS: Don't be too quick to react that you forget to question your thoughts. Questioning your thoughts and asking yourself why you want to react the way you want to, helps you find the right words to express yourself. It makes you think before reacting. This is a calmer way to handle situations.

- RESPOND: After careful questioning and thinking, you can finally respond to the situation in the best way you can.

Practice the daily tips for the maintenance of your wellbeing. This will help you attend to all aspects of your wellbeing. When no part of your wellbeing is neglected, you live healthily and quality lives just like an IT Girl.

7

SHE'S INTO
HIGH QUALITY

High-Quality Is Not A Luxury To Us. It's A Necessity.

– IT GIRL LUXURY

The IT Girl lifestyle is all about high quality in every part of our lives. This means indulging only in high-quality foods, high-quality relationships, high-quality clothing, high-quality friendships, high-quality experiences, and so forth. We know that in this world many times (not all the time) higher quality things cost money. If you are working your way to enjoying and occupying your time with just higher quality overall experiences while being mindful of your money, we always advise for you to take your time and invest. Everything doesn't need to be done at once. You will gradually be able to invest in all these areas of your life that involve money because quality is not only a degree of excellence that meets and exceeds expectations but also last a long period of time. So let's explore what that looks like.

High-Quality Foods

IT Girls love high-quality foods. Whether you are the one making it or someone else is making it, what you put in your body matters in terms of how your muscles, heart, blood cells, and brain function. When you choose to put high-quality foods in your body, you have a sense of awareness for yourself. High-quality food is considered unrefined, minimally processed foods such as fruits and vegetables, whole grains, healthy fats, and healthy sources of protein. Eating quality foods not only helps you to function better, but also helps you to feel better about yourself. When you are truly aware of what you put into your body, this, in turn, becomes a reflection of the other ways that you look out for yourself. High-quality foods are important for energy, wellness, outward appearance as well as lung and organ functionality. High-quality foods play a big part in your quality of life. We know that indulging in other foods from time to time is more than okay but IT Girls make it a priority to eat as healthy as possible whenever possible.

If you are just starting your journey of becoming an IT Girl, you will realize that converting everything around you may take some time and effort to get used to but it can be done. You can go cold turkey and decide right now to get rid of everything and anything that is not high-quality food or gradually evolve in this process by doing an inventory of the snacks you eat and then looking into what you eat when you are in a rush and for convenience. We're not saying to give up everything now (unless you can do that, then go for it) but to start to make the changes as this is necessary for demanding quality in your life. From the foods you purchase to put in your fridge to the foods you choose when you go out to eat, always choose quality. Even when there are times when you may want to indulge in fast food, you want to be aware of the kinds of fast food you are eating. For example, if you are eating fried chicken, you want to be sure that the chicken you are eating is real chicken. Even if you choose to be vegan, be a healthy vegan. Eating french fries and chips each day is not considered quality nor being a healthy vegan.

Start to only accept quality and you will notice that you will only receive quality.

High-Quality Clothing

We talk a lot about fashion, designers, and well luxury. We love luxury. We often notice that many confuse designer luxury brands with high quality. While at one point in time designer luxury brands were synonymous with high quality, we currently cannot agree with that today as we have noticed a few designers taking shortcuts with the materials being used to save money. While we can go on about this (and soon we will), the point is for you to be aware that all designer luxury brands are not and/or have not kept up with quality and there are many lesser-known brands that produce high-quality clothing. But before you start ditching all your clothes for only designer luxury brands that produce higher quality pieces, please be aware of the material that your clothing items are made from. There are several brands that will have you paying top dollar just for polyester. We highly encourage you to stay away from such material. This is what we mean when we say to be aware.

When we talk about high-quality clothing we are talking about how it feels on you, its durability, and the wash and wear of the material. You want to invest in high-quality pieces especially when it comes to your basics because you want them to last a long time. You want clothes that are built to last and clothing made with materials such as cotton, linen, merino wool, cashmere, hemp, and silk which are all considered high-quality materials. Avoid clothing that is made with polyester, rayon, acetate, nylon, and over 50% acrylic (which are all man-made fabrics). Thick material garments, as well as handcrafted garments, are what we look for in quality clothing. Here are some other things to look for when considering purchasing clothing...

- TIGHT STITCHING. What we mean by this is being able to pull and stretch your clothing item without seeing any gaps when you pull at the seams.

- SPEAKING OF SEAMS WE MEAN FABRIC PATTERN MATCHING AT THE SEAMS. When it does match this is just an indication of more time and material spent to make sure the clothing item you picked happens to be of quality. Many clothing manufacturers know this takes more time and material and will skip this part.

- WHEN IT COMES TO DENIM WE RECOMMEND FEELING IF IT IS HEAVY AND MAYBE EVEN STIFF. High-quality denim feels heavy because of the material's thread count. The cheaper denim does feel softer because they contain fewer fibers and are prewashed with chemicals to achieve that softness which decreases its durability. This is according to GQ.

- SEE-THROUGH MATERIALS ARE USUALLY A SIGN THAT THEY ARE NOT BUILT TO LAST. Sheer materials are usually very prone to tearing.

We want you to stay away from fabrics such as polyester, satin, nylon, and rayon as they can restrict your skin from breathing, can clog pores, and even cause rashes. High-quality clothing should not do these things to your skin. Skin is our largest organ and treating it well as well as protecting it is important. What you wear that lays on your skin matters. So fabrics such as wool (not softer merino wool) can trigger eczema flare-ups and irritate normal skin. But by far the worst fabric for your skin is polyester. There are so many reasons why this is a 'stay away fabric' but we do suggest that you stay away from it if you want to invest and build a collection of high-quality pieces that will last a long time. Not only can your skin not breathe with polyester but it also traps in odors and creates an environment for smelly bacteria to grow because of skin germs found in sweat that the fibers can't absorb. Be conscious of the labels and clothing you choose to invest in for your health and durability.

High-Quality Friendships

When you don't play about yourself, you don't allow others to play with you either.

The kinds of friends that you have around you play a role in your life. While you may be repeating to yourself that your quality of life is what matters and everything within your life is of high quality, ask yourself if your friendships at this point are. You may keep a small tight circle of friends or have a large circle of friends, but whatever the size of your circle of friends, ask yourself about the quality of your circle. Realize that each friend plays a different role in your life but do each of these friends contain positive attributes that make it worth continuing hopefully a lifelong friendship with them? Okay so let's take a quick look at some of the positive traits of a great friend.

Great friends....

- Are Dependable
- Are Individuals You Can Trust
- Have Morals And Values And Live With Integrity
- Are Empathetic
- Typically Share The Same Interest
- Are Loyal
- Allow You To Be Yourself While They Can Be Themselves
- Do Not Pass Judgement
- Can Give You Constructive Criticism
- Make Time For You
- Show Up For You And Support You
- Always Have Your Best Interest In Mind
- They Understand When You Say No To Something
- They Make You Feel Safe Through Life Challenges
- They Honor Your Boundaries
- Respect Your Differences
- Are Positive Individuals Also Working On Themselves
- Always Want The Best For You
- Can Apologize When They Are Wrong

These are just a few positive traits of what we consider a good quality friend around you has. Understand if your friend does not have any of these qualities ii you find yourself making excuses for why they treat you the way they do, then they may not currently be the friend you need around you right now in your life. High-quality friendships are important because they can help bring more happiness into our lives. These people that you call your friends have a huge impact on your mental health, physical health, and happiness. With the right group of friends, you should feel less stressed, more hopeful, extremely confident, no longer isolated or lonely and have a sense of joy and fun. When you want to get away from it all or need someone to talk to, your friends should be there for you and vice versa. Your conversations should be about improving your well-being and finding opportunities to increase your quality of life and simply having fun. When you have the right friends, anything you are struggling with you should struggle less with and even act as an accountability partner for whatever you are trying to achieve. Your friends should want the absolute best for you and even pray for you when needed. They help you reach your dreams while helping you gain self-discipline. For example, a friend who knows you have been working on starting your own business and been at it night and day to present to an important customer/partner would never force you to attend a party that takes away your focus and doesn't help you build connections. This friend would understand your goals and respect the current boundaries you have in place for yourself.

It's never too late to make friends in life. We do not care if you are a mother that is twenty-two or a fifty-two year young woman. With an amazing personality and the natural IT Girl you are becoming, making new friends with different individuals from all aspects of life will never be a challenge for you because as an IT Girl you automatically assume that it is natural for you to have the right individuals enchanted by you and wanting to be your friend. We do want to say stay away from friends who talk to you about their other friends or your other friends because eventually, you will negatively become the topic of conversation. Stay away from jealous individuals. Individuals who do not believe in you. Individuals who wonder why great things happen for you and not them. Individuals who do not try to pull you up when you are down and have betrayed your trust. Stay away from individuals who have no morals and those whom you have seen smile in others' faces but have done unpleasant things behind their backs. Stay away from narcissists and those who belittle you and bully you. These types of individuals do not bring anything of quality to you but hard learning lessons that we want you to avoid.

Believe us when we say high-quality friendships can change the whole trajectory of your life. You will never settle for less in a friendship knowing what a great friend is and how a great friend is supposed to show up in your life.

High-Quality Relationships

We spoke about friendships, but now let's take a look at our relationships. These relationships can be with our parents, our significant others, and so forth. What kind of relationships are we maintaining? When we are involved in an intimate relationship with another individual, this is the person that gets to see all of us (for the most part) and we get to see all of them. We spoke before about how you talk to yourself, but now ask yourself how do they talk to you. How do they view you and treat you? How are you learning and growing within your relationships? Are you being loved, cared for, nurtured, freely given affection, easily given grace, and ultimately feeling fulfilled in the relationship? Are you being respected and allowed to be your authentic self? Is this an empowering relationship or one that is draining and feels like a second full-time job? Are you providing all the care but not feeling like it is being reciprocated?

We all need meaningful connections that are critical for our health and happiness but are you truly receiving that with the relationships you currently have? If you are not feeling valued, supported, and have a sense of belonging then it's time to reevaluate what you are in. Can you communicate your feelings without having to feel guilty for feeling them? How you are being treated matters, and IT Girls do not put up with situations where we are disrespected and feel like we are being demeaned. The quality of your relationships plays a big role in the quality of your life. High-quality relationships are where two people put in the effort to be there for each other and prioritize the relationship to keep it from deteriorating. Understand that the person that you choose to have an intimate relationship with is extremely important. This person knowingly and unknowingly will influence so many of your decisions with money, happiness, family, friends, your life journey and so much more. You want to make sure that this person brings out the best in you, not the worst within you. The person you choose to be in a relationship with should make your life easier and provide a sense of joy.

When it comes to your parents, well this could be tricky. If you have a great relationship with your parents we say congratulations! But if you do not have a great relationship with your parents then you can either try to work on having a better relationship with them or keep your distance. Now we are not encouraging the easy route nor are we encouraging toxic relationships, but what we are saying is if your relationship with your parent(s) has a shot at improving (to where you and your parent can work on having a much more fulfilling relationship with each other) then do it. Drop the ego and learn to lead with love and positivity if you are holding on to something. If you simply have parents who are determined to disrespect you, degrade you, and refuse to change, then it's time to step away from what you are used to by letting go of the hope to change them and just focusing on you and living in your bubble of positivity. Make a promise to yourself that you will work on yourself and only choose high-quality two-sided relationships.

High-Quality Experiences

When the student is ready the teacher will appear
— Tao Te Ching

What makes life feel so good and makes others want to be an IT Girl is her experiences. We each have amazing 'wow' moments in our lives where we may have felt some kind of love, attention, or just simply cared for. When you hear another IT Girl's story of an experience she just so much enjoyed and went through, most of the time you are in awe of her favor. You are enamored by the attention that she may have received in her experience that may have seemed personalized just for her. This is because IT Girls set themselves up and expect high-quality experiences. It is not outside of you but one you simply are. When you are in essence 'a high-quality experience' for another (inspiring them to want to be better in themselves) then it's only natural to expect high-quality experiences as something you are. IT Girls typically encounter high-quality experiences because they don't compartmentalize themselves. We do not let small decisions hold us back from the experiences we would like to have. We do not limit our thoughts to what we think we know that tells us we can't. IT Girls follow their instincts and understand the logic of some of their decisions later. Now we're not saying to do things like jump into the water knowing you can't swim or anything crazy like that. We are saying instinctively you will know where to go and what to do when you are in tune with your IT Girl self and follow it. Life is to be experienced and having the right attitude to experience it most amazingly will get you to where we believe you will feel amazing and fulfilled. You will find purpose. You will view life with such happiness and greater gratitude.

And with all that we spoke about with having high-quality experiences, we have to say that the IT Girls that have the most amazing high-quality experiences are not only open but also passionate.

That's right. IT Girls are extremely passionate about something. Now we know you may be thinking 'but what if I do not have anything I am passionate about' but we want you to know that there is something out there that you truly really care about on a passionate level. Maybe you tried to take the time to figure out what it was but simply couldn't figure it out. We say that is okay, but we know you will in time be able to find out what it is and even redefine what the word passionate means to you. In general, passion means to show or be caused by a strong feeling, strong belief, and/or an intense feeling towards something. High-quality experiences are translated to our ears as passionate experiences that evoke an amazing feeling that you will never forget.

If you have several things that you are passionate about then congratulations on achieving one of the many steps that would help generate a purpose that you can evolve in. But if you currently do not have something you are passionate about, let us help you in discovering it.

So first while we never believe in focusing on the things you feel like you lack, this is the one time we would say let's take a closer look in that area. Now when we say let's take a look at what you may feel you may be lacking, we aren't talking about exterior things like long hair or fewer freckles. Even though if you choose to look at that we could get deeper and say maybe you may find passion in beautiful things and even want to create or work alongside beautiful things. What we mean when we say let's take a closer look at what you may feel like you lack in, we mean let's look at things that we may desire and want. This could be things such as love (we'll use this as an example). You may even feel cynical about love because of your past experiences or because you just haven't had the love that the hopeless romantics keep talking about and expressing. If you keep thinking about love and when love will come your way, what love looks like, and what being loved properly means to you, then you can start right there and say you have a high interest in this area not only because you feel like you may not have it, but because of how it makes you feel and how you would feel if you were to have it. You can take it even a step further and say it may not even be the love in itself that interest you but all the actions that come with love and what you have a high interest in showing and receiving. This is something that you could explore and have a high-quality experience in. This would mean so much to you and when felt and experienced you would share it with others who would then feel the intensity of what you are saying and view it as a 'wow,' that was a custom for her type of experience. Of course, the same can be said for the opposite of this and so forth. Think about it. Those who fight love off so much and talk badly about it but in reality are just waiting for an experience that would take away all the negativity that has been felt, so they can let go of the battle of what they thought they were fighting to only experience it in the most pleasurable way. It then becomes something they are passionate about expressing and keeping.

When we say IT Girls are passionate we mean it. You can be passionate about several things. You can be passionate about something and change your mind about it a few years later. There is no limit in passion nor any limitation in quality experiences.

While we mentioned a few areas in your life that you would want to make sure that is of high quality, we know there are so many more areas in your life that could be of higher quality. These areas may even need a drastic makeover to get the kind of high-quality aspect that you want. Take the time to transform the different areas in your life into a crystal clear high-quality way of living and being. We IT Girls indulge in high-quality lifestyles thus the reason why we always want others to live with us in our cloud nine.

8

THE FOUR TYPES OF FEMALE FRIENDS YOU NEED IN YOUR LIFE

Let's Get Into Friendships

Friendships are very important aspects of our lives. Even our mental health is affected by the impact of our friendships. The type of friends we have, also tells a lot about us. Everyone wants a strong friendship, but not everyone will put in all the efforts needed to build a strong friendship. While some people find it easy to make friends, some battle with making friends, and some others find it is easy to meet new people but they never have the energy to sustain the friendship. However, not all friendships are worth our time, but some are worth fighting with every ounce of our strength.

Who Are Real Friends?

While we somewhat covered this earlier, real friends are people you can always rely on no matter what happens. They stand up for you even when no one is watching and they encourage you to achieve your goals. A real friend is someone you can count on and someone who accepts you for who you are. IT Girls are big on friendships. We value friendships and also believe in having a small circle (like we said before large circles are good too if they work for you). To us, quality is much better than quantity any time any day. Genuine friendships involve a level of intimacy. IT Girls are women that are there for their friends, even amid storms. We value friendships and invest in them too.

The Four Types Of Female Friends
You Need In Your Life

We all have different types of friends, but there are four special types of friends you need in your life. These friends possess the ultimate best friend characteristics. Great friends exist and when you have them, hold on to them tightly because they are rare to come by.

1. THE SOUL SISTER: This type of friend can sense when something is wrong without your telling her. She is like family and you are both like sisters. She is always there for you and sometimes you can't imagine life without her.

2. THE OUTSPOKEN FRIEND: This type of friend is bold enough to say what's on her mind. She tells you the truth to your face, no matter how hard it hurts. She lets you know when you are wrong and is not afraid to keep it real. But the good thing about this type of friend is that she is bold enough to stand up for you and is ever ready to defend you.

3. THE INSPIRING FRIEND: This type of friend motivates and inspires you to become a better version of yourself. She says little, but her actions are enough motivation for you.

4. THE CONFIDANT FRIEND: This doesn't mean that you don't trust all your friends, but you trust this particular friend more. You feel very comfortable sharing your secrets with her and you are sure that no other ear would hear of it. Trustworthy friends like her should be held tightly.

The Types Of Friends To Avoid

Some friendships can be draining and should be avoided by all means. Here are a few types of friends to avoid.

1. THE GOSSIP FRIEND: This friend finds it easy talking badly about other people. Everyone except her has a problem. Avoid this type of friend because the day she talks about you, you're finished!

2. THE ENERGY DRAINING FRIEND: This type of friend is only after what you give them, and you gain nothing from being friends with them. Staying with them consistently becomes draining for you because when once you are done having conversations with them, you are in low spirits and a sad mood. It is like a parasitic relationship.

3. THE FRIEND THAT KEEP RECORD: Now don't get us wrong. Some good friends keep a record of the good times just for memory's sake, but some friends keep a record of how you treat them. This friend calculates to know if you both are giving the same energy in the friendship and sometimes they do things not because they want to do them but because they want to measure up so that everything will be equal. This type of friend also keeps a record of who does the most or who wrongs the most. It can be draining because the beauty of the actual friendship is not seen. It merely becomes a race to catch up with each other's friendship deeds.

4. THE FAIR-WEATHER FRIEND: This friend only sticks with you when the going is good. When things get rough, she is nowhere to be seen. Some friends are only there because of the attention you get. They get close to you to also get that same attention. They never really care about you. They only care about what they stand to gain by being your friend.

5. THE PROBLEM FRIEND: This type of friend only needs you because she is going through a problem. After that, she forgets you. She never cares to know if you have your problems too and she is also never ready to listen to you, even if you have a problem.

Realizing The Friendships That You Need To Let Go

When you have the type of friend that you ought to avoid and you have tried to talk to them about the problem in the friendship but they are not willing to see things from your point of view, then it's time to call it quits with the friendship.

It might be hard to let go of some friendships (especially those that have lasted for years) but there are reasons you should let go of such friendships. Here are a few friendships you need to let go of.

1. FRIENDS THAT ONLY FOCUS ON THE NEGATIVE SIDE OF YOU. This type of friend makes you feel bad about yourself. It could be that they are jealous of all the good things you have and they talk negatively about you so that you don't feel good about yourself, either. No one likes to have jealous friends around them, or do you?

2. FRIENDS THAT DON'T VALUE FRIENDSHIP: Some friends are not ready to be there for you. They are only there for the gains and when you start having it rough; they flee.

3. FRIENDS THAT AREN'T HONEST WITH YOU: These friends are not trustworthy and you feel insecure sharing things about yourself with them.

4. FRIENDSHIPS WHERE YOU SEEM TO BE THE ONLY ONE PUTTING IN THE EFFORT: This can be draining; being the person that does everything to fix the problems in your friendships, being the person that is always there for the other person, and not having some of your friendship deeds reciprocated. It is okay if your friend doesn't give in as much as you give in your friendship, but it isn't okay when you are the only one acting as the pillar of the friendship. You aren't the only one in the friendship. Both of you ought to be there for each other too.

5. FRIENDS THAT DON'T VALUE YOU: When you are around people that don't value you and your opinion, you start to think that you are not

good enough. You should be around friends who are ready to support and encourage you towards achieving your goals. Friends who would hype you up.

6. FRIENDS THAT ARE TOO NEEDY.

7. FRIENDS THAT BEAR GRUDGES.

Letting go of friendships might be a hard decision for you to make but you must realize that not everyone is meant to stay in our lives forever. Some people are in our lives to simply serve specific purposes and once the purpose is achieved, there is no point in holding on to the friendship because it starts to become draining.

The Female Code Of Friendships

These are the unwritten rules about friendships that exist amongst women. They are those commandments that govern friendships between women. They are like the dos and don'ts of friendships.

Do not expose your friend's secret to other people after your friend has confided in you.

Confront your friend about issues that didn't sit well with you but don't go about telling other people that care to listen without confronting your friend first.

If your friend is seeking your opinion about something, be honest and tell them what you think about it; be it their style, make-up, or hairdo. Kindly do this and suggest other options. Don't try to please your friend by not being truthful in situations like this.

Never go after your friend's ex. Your friend's ex is off-limits. Your friend ended her relationship with him for a reason and you shouldn't make her start to remember things about her past relationship by dating her ex.

Tell your friend if her partner is cheating on her. Always be on the lookout for your friend in whatever way you can.

These unspoken rules are made to support one another as women and to also genuinely look out for others. While you make decisions regarding your friendships, always remember that strong friendships are not built in a day.

9

UNDERSTANDING THE
MYSTERY OF AN IT GIRL
AND HOW TO CREATE
AND BUILD YOUR MYSTERY

Like most IT Girls, there is always a bit of mystery surrounding her. She has an electrifying personality that captures the imagination of millions. Our aura around ourselves comprises of how we speak, walk, move our bodies, style, look, how we react, and do what we do. We IT Girls captivate the world's attention and capture the hearts of many. There are many theories about us IT Girls and who we are and we are sure you becoming one have a bit of that mystery around yourself.

Here are a few facts about IT Girls. We are strong, beautiful women who know our worth and are not often taken for granted by those who appreciate our magnetic energy. We love intensely and our smile is infectious. We do not talk a lot whenever we speak because we know that our words are impactful and heard by many. We speak in ways that make others feel like they know a bit about us without actually knowing much about us. We value keeping certain things private and sacred to us.

The real mystery of an IT Girl as you can see is just not revealing everything while still being yourself. An IT Girl knows how to use discretion and continues to be a positive light no matter where she is in life. She is full of gratitude and love. It's the mystery that always has others wondering. The thing about mystery is that it isn't done on purpose. This is just who she is. You don't have to purposely start your day by saying how am I going to give off the mystery? No that is not it. When you value certain things and live your life as the main character romanticizing every part of it, the mystery just naturally happens because what you are focused on most that are watching are not focused on that. They are focused on you. And what you are focused on always tends to be somewhat sacred anyways.

So when we talk about how to create and build on your mystery the answer is quite simple. Continue to view yourself as the main character and focus on what interest you, making sure that what you focus on and give your attention to isn't tied to a person who can change the way you view life and your happiness. You make moves towards your new journey of the goals you have created for yourself. You do not compromise your happiness or your commitments just to please others.

In general, you can create mystery by simply not documenting everything on social media, by not accepting every invitation presented to you, often staying neutral, and not responding in group conversations unless spoken to directly (your prettiness speaks loud enough). This doesn't mean not to speak up when necessary, it means knowing when to do so. When you do speak, speak with authority. This means clearly and effectively. Not loud and rushed.

There are a few ways you can create effortless mystery with different people in your life. We broke down a few ways that you can do this and for it to naturally become who you are.

Being Seen As Mysterious Around Your Partner

When it comes to being in a relationship with someone, a sense of mystery is always welcomed and needed in a relationship. When things become too predictable, it is easy to be taken for granted. So you can start creating mystery about yourself by being more assertive. Oh we know this sounds a bit weird but trust us, this is one way to do it. Whenever you are asked what you want, actually know what you want. Now you can ask how does that build mystery? Well if you are the person who always says I don't know or even returns the question with the same question, all of the sudden you knowing what you want whenever asked will raise some eyebrows. No longer wait for your partner to ask. Always state you need this or you would like that and so forth. It makes it clear that you are an IT Girl that means business when it comes to anything about you. But let's take this a step further, mystery does not necessarily mean hiding. When it comes to having a bit of mystery in your relationship with your partner we like to say master the art of saying less while giving the information that needs to be given in the most positive way. So what does this look like? Well, an example of this would be initiating a date night without giving too much of the details and asking him questions he would be interested in while speaking less about you. End the date with him feeling amazing and leaving him to wonder more about you. He would feel like he knows so much but really doesn't know much information about where you are headspace-wise. Now do this when you are confident in yourself and truly in a relationship you are happy with. Do not use this tactic as a way to manipulate an individual for selfish reasons. This should be a genuine act.

Another way you can be seen as mysterious to your partner is by breaking away from your daily routine to do something different. Spending some time apart and of course, keep some things private like bodily functions (if this is your cup of tea). Learn how to be direct and not give an unnecessary explanation. Relax on the constant texting and oversharing of your feelings. Always stating how you feel when you aren't even being asked (this is different from demanding what you want in what we previously stated) actually steals the experience of your partner getting to know more about you on their own. So with this, we say chill out and hold back on trying to learn everything so quickly and revealing so much too soon.

One thing an IT Girl is always doing is actively pursuing her passion in ways that are authentic to her and don't have her life revolving around her relationship. This naturally creates mystery around you with your partner.

Creating A Bit Of Mystery With Family Members

As an IT Girl, you may already be a little bit of a mystery to your family. But if you feel that you are lacking the respect that you should be experiencing with family members, it is probably because they are too accessible to you and quite honestly feel like they know so much about you because of their access to you. The first way to create a bit of mystery with your family would be in keeping your distance from certain family members and limit what you say. This is important because family are good at triggers and have no problem triggering you to act out of character. While we covered this in discussing cutting back on negative and toxic energy, it's important to note that protecting yourself does create a sense of mystery. We also say keep your answers short and don't feel obligated to explain anything. It doesn't matter if you disagree with something or have a different point of view towards something that happened now or in the past. Keeping your responses short will have family members possibly trying to ask more questions to get you to expand and this would be your opportunity to always keep it brief. Whenever there is a family function, leave early. Not only does this create a bit of mystery but the mystery can help you build a certain level of respect because it shows that you put yourself first. It will convey the message that you are not obligated to my time (if in a toxic family environment) and start to give a higher level of respect for the times you do choose to show up. Remember that with family members, the work is different because there is an obligation to make a special effort while creating a space just for yourself.

Being Mysterious Around Your Coworkers

When it comes to work, there are many different personalities and surprisingly being the mysterious IT Girl at work is actually pretty easy and comes with a few advantages. Let's start with your personal style. You'll always capture attention with the care you give to your attire. Dressing the IT Girl way will always get you noticed and your mannerisms will always have people wondering. Being mysterious at work also helps with keeping a bit of distance where you don't have to reveal much about yourself. If you want to keep things just professional you can do so and if you would like to connect with certain people at work who can help you maneuver your way around your career field. We love to say don't give away too much. What we mean is that everyone should not know everything about your life. You can do an amazing job, smile, and have conversations but learning when to exit a conversation early enough so it doesn't get into your personal life is a skill. You can also establish a bit of mystery by being successful at what you do and doing it well because many will want to know how you make things happen and how you tell them (if you tell them) will make them feel like you said a lot without them knowing. When you make everything just seem like it is just effortless to you, you create mystery and become the 'go-to person' for just about anything. People will go out of their way to talk to you without having much to say just so they can interact with you. Regardless of how much you would want to talk about something personal, you will always want to have a bit of mystery around you that keeps people talking and admiring you with awe. You'll soon become one of if not the most interesting woman in your work area.

Being Mysterious Around Your Friends

Sometimes even with your friends, you have to leave a little bit of mystery and the main way to do that is by having self-confidence. Whatever you are doing with your friends, always be yourself. Never act or try too hard. Being confident is a way that tells everyone how amazing you are. Be proud of who you are and what makes you unique. When you don't try too hard, don't care about what others think, move how you want, do things your way (the way that is right for you) and not follow the crowd because that is just what everyone else is doing then you love yourself right into main character mode and operate from that. You do not care whether people like you or do not like you because you do what is best for you in the decisions you make for yourself (of course this means making decisions that don't harm others). Confidence here is the key to the mystery within friendships.

Being Mysterious Around Strangers

Well, this is easily said that you are already a mystery simply because the people who are strangers to you do not know you. But to turn up the mystery knob a notch some of the things to bring in the right kind of mystery is always having eye contact. Not just any contact but you know the smize eye contact. A smize means to smile with your eyes. Be warm and welcoming with your eyes. Another thing is to always look amazing and always have a good time. Everyone is attracted to the IT Girl who looks like she is having a good time and looks amazing doing it. Think about social media. When you are posting pictures of yourself how are you conveying yourself and what kind of mystery do you think is forming from it? You shouldn't be so conscious of how you look when doing certain things and talking to people but you should just be and it will naturally show.

Being mysterious is something you can naturally be with just a few things to keep in mind. Most IT Girls are wonderful with the art of mystery and always keep you wanting more from them in some way, shape, or fashion. In the end when you see other IT Girls be inspired by them but create your sense of mystery because IT Girls can be anything and everything while being the ultimate enigma. The complete secret to building mystery is confidence. A woman who knows her power will always be this mysterious woman in the best way of the word to everyone around her (even the ones who claim to know her). So no matter how old or young we are or where we are in our lives, we have something that many want to know about but we must learn to keep to ourselves and cherish.

Having Your Own Hobbies

What is so nice about someone with a natural sense of mystery is finding out little pieces of information about them a little at a time. The same thing can be said about you. We encourage you to have hobbies that you truly enjoy doing. These are activities that either keep you active, help you to relax and have fun, grow you in some aspect or naturally interest you. Hobbies look different to everyone. It can be something as simple as reading, traveling, collecting stamps, cooking, or anything else you can think of. While we spoke about being passionate earlier, these activities could be something you're passionate about but don't have to be. Remember that hobbies are what you do in your free time that brings you joy. This is typically something you are interested in and committed to and is part of your mystery when someone finds out about your hobby. Spending time engaging in a hobby creates more depth about you and allows you to focus more on developing yourself rather than being everywhere and not minding your own business to where you are easily accessible. Being easily accessible takes away from the art of your mystery.

You must know that being mysterious isn't something that is limited to age. As we stated at the beginning of this book, IT Girls are women of any age bracket. So your mystery can run from your twenties to your seventies or start in your forties or even in your thirties. IT Girls are deemed as 'unattainable' at any age because you can't just put them in a box. She lets her looks, walk, and voice build magic. IT Girls have a level of high self-confidence in themselves and in their sexuality which makes her comfortable with who she is. We are not standoffish. So the physical grace that comes with the mystery of an IT Girl is easy to notice and one that is admired by many. IT Girls are authentic to themselves and others. There is nothing forced or faked which gives so much to be admired in a world that has a lot of that going on. She is a sense of possibility and adventure in life. She is mindful and intentional about the decisions she makes, and takes full ownership of her life rather than let other people define it. The mystery is not about hiding or pretending but about just being and knowing.

10

HOW AN IT GIRL COMMUNICATES

Let's Talk Communication

Communication is big and we definitely communicate in many different ways. From verbal to body language to even written, we as IT Girls know the importance of the way we communicate with others. Communication is something we must talk about because this is how we can get what we want, express our boundaries, make others around us feel great, and so forth. Not everything needs to be said with your words and not everything can be said with a text message. Sometimes one look says it all. When we speak about communication we want you to think about how do you communicate best. What aspect of yourself needs to be worked on? What do you always tend to try to communicate about yourself the most? When it comes to expressing yourself there are several ways to be able to do so to get what you want. Let's give a couple of scenarios:

Let's say your partner has come home from work and has had a bad day. You want him to be open to something that you would like him to do or you may even want him to calm down and relax. What would be the best way to deal with a situation like this?

Our answer: Sit down with him real close. Let him talk if he is talking while looking him in the eye the whole time. Gently caress his arm and while doing so you should continue to be attentive and let him talk. Even if his voice is elevated and he is angry do not match his energy but rather let him conform to yours. When you have an opportunity to talk (never cutting him off) you look him in the eye and in a very soft but meaningful voice tell him you understand or compliment him on how he handled whatever the situation was. Then continue to say well I believe…. Or say I would like it if you …. all doing this by being gentle but authoritative and yet attentive and understanding. You used body language and verbal communication to state what you want and turn the tone and attitude of his around to get what you want and what he probably wants and needs. This will make your partner want to listen to you more. You want to always want to make someone feel heard and validated. Always be in your feminine energy and communicate only from that place.

Let's look at another scenario:

You are at work and it is time for your evaluation. You want to present the idea of getting a raise at this time. Being an IT Girl, that shouldn't be too hard for you but you would like to communicate the kind of raise or position that you want and the perks that you want with that. How would you go about doing this?

Our answer: All discussions for advancement in the workplace should be done face to face always sitting down. When you sit down do not sit two or three seats away. One seat away is fine. The reason for this is to keep it professional while building a connection and not making this seem so formal to bring down the person's guard. Being seated away automatically makes it extremely formal and gives the other person time to turn down the request. When you are being evaluated let the other person speak first by saying to them 'I would love to hear how you feel I have contributed to the company' or 'I would like to hear....' Then you let them talk. You let them talk without ever interrupting them and looking at them softly with understanding in the eyes but of course with a bit of authority. After they have finished talking acknowledge what was said by saying I hear everything you've said. I understand when you said ...... then with your feminine soft authority state what you have done and how you have brought value and where the company was before and where it is now because of your contributions. But when you do this do not give an attitude. If you feel like you have to fight for your position remember that and continue to stay in your strong but soft feminine state. Be sure to state what you appreciate about the company and thank them for your growth. Regardless of what is said, you know your value so do not be moved to over-explain yourself or get upset by what is said (if it is unfavorable), but continue to always hold your position as the IT Girl you are. We believe that you would receive a favorable outcome and if not, we suggest taking it a step further and communicating through a formal written letter covering your evaluation experience, what you felt, and your ultimate desire for it. Through this method of communication, we believe as an IT Girl you will get your desired result (given that you meet and have fulfilled other requirements needed to get what you are requesting).

Let's discuss being in disagreements. IT Girls do not argue with others. You may have a disagreement from time to time and may even have to learn to pick your battles when voicing your opinions, but full-blown arguments with individuals are not something that we engage with. Why because we do not allow anyone to pull us into that space. We can effectively communicate our thoughts without screaming, name-calling, and cursing someone and something out. The way we communicate with people is always being watched by others. The way you respond to things that are made to get some kind of reaction from you is there to test you and get you out of character. It is a setup to say this is who you really are. Realize that how you react is more important than what you say when you are reacting out of character. Most people will describe how you act before stating the things you said. IT Girls are aware of the motive and do not participate unless for a good cause like a protest or using their voice for influence and even then IT Girls are great at articulating their thoughts and feelings.

Never Raise Your Voice And Only Say It One Time To Make Sure You Are Heard

You should never have to raise your voice and you should only have to convey your message one time to make sure that you are heard. As an IT Girl, you are highly respected and many people want to hear what you have to say the first time. But for those special times where your audience is the same and it seems that you have to repeat yourself for a second or third time, we want to tell you to stop that. If they missed it the first time then they missed it. By repeating yourself over and over again, you are teaching others that they do not have to listen the first time that you talk. When speaking, always make eye contact with the person you are speaking to, and do not break that eye contact until that person understands you. If you are on the phone or in person, wait until the atmosphere is quiet before you start talking. If you get a response like 'what?' do not follow up by repeating yourself. Simply stay quiet because they more than likely heard you and are just trying to sort out what they heard. Of course assuming you are speaking in a volume that they can hear you clearly and it is directed to them, the best way to not have to repeat yourself and command what you want and/or convey your message is after you are done speaking, ask the receiver of the message if the message was received with authority in a posture and tone that is not desperate but one that says got it?

You do not need to run someone down with questions and commands. Command attention and be heard by teaching others around you how to listen to you. Let it be known that what you say is important because you may not speak much but when you do speak it is important and you will be heard. It is in this way you never have to raise your voice to be heard because people are waiting to hear what you have to say. People know that what you speak is meaningful and filled with some kind of wisdom that promotes clarity and some sort of happiness. We hear you and know that they will hear you too.

11

IT GIRL ETIQUETTE

IT Girls are feminine women whose etiquette practices have made them stand out. Feminine women stand out because of the way they talk, walk, use gestures, speech tones, and good manners. All of these are traits that other people find irresistible. Being feminine can be mistaken for being unnatural but really, it's all about naturally displaying grace even amid storms. Acting well-mannered makes you charming and elegant. Having etiquette is having a set of rules that guide your behavior in different situations. IT Girls know how to live life with sophistication while still being a bit out of the box and different. In all of this, we stay true to ourselves and live in moderation.

To be in touch with your feminine essence, let's look into the fifteen etiquette practices of IT Girls.

Fifteen Feminine Women Etiquette Practices

Remember, IT Girls do not practice these etiquettes only when they go to events. It is part of our daily lifestyles. It shows that we value other people as much as we value ourselves. This is also one of the secrets to our successful lifestyles. It makes us respond in the right way to situations.

1. WALK: Feminine women walk softly. We take short light steps that are elegant. The gentle and comfortable strides that we take give us a level of confidence. Make it natural and practice taking gentle steps daily.

2. GESTURES: IT Girls are not known for too many gesticulations. We are known to express ourselves with ease without having to use different hand gestures.

3. TONE: Your tone of voice should be soothing and gentle. We speak softly and properly. Being loud doesn't mean people will listen to you.

4. STANCE: We stand straight with relaxed shoulders, tucked-in bellies, and feet that are close to each other. It builds our level of confidence too.

5. SIT: While sitting on low chairs, we do not cross our legs. We hold our knees together by leaning them to the side.

6. SMILE: This is one of our charming qualities. Smiling doesn't cost a thing except for your cheek muscles of course! We do not act wildly in public. We comport ourselves and grin when necessary.

7. FACIAL EXPRESSIONS: The facial expressions of IT Girls are heartwarming. Sometimes we use our faces to speak. Your facial expression reflects your character sometimes. Also, your state of mind is reflected on your face. When you're tired, stressed, sleepy, or excited, it will all show in your facial expressions. Hence to try to be more relaxed, try to manage stress well, and get good sleep too.

8. WE SPEAK LESS AND LISTEN MORE: IT Girls are good listeners. In this way, we show respect to others by letting them know that we not only value them but respect their opinions too. While holding conversations with people, we pay attention and keep our phones aside. We show genuine interest and carefully listen to all that they have to say. Indeed, you don't have to agree with everything someone else has to say, but you can always express yourself politely and respectfully disagree. We steer clear of gossip because we know how hurtful it feels to say untrue things about others in their absence. We do not engage in any form of negative talk but rather we do when needed constructively criticize people.

9. IN STATE OF LANGOUR: Feminine women know how to control their moods. We appear calm even when we are tired or going through a hard time.

10. SPEECH: We talk with love and kindness. In our speeches, we are polite. We also speak with confidence and walk with calm poise. We do not use swear or vulgar words.

11. WELL-MANNERED: We treat others with kindness, respect, and affection. Saying thank you, sorry, please and other polite words are ways we are being genuinely kind to others. There is beauty in kindness. Sending a thank you note to someone that helped you a long time ago is a good way to start with this etiquette practice.

12. NOT BEING SHOWY: We are not ones to dress provocatively. Feminine women dress appropriately. Wearing too much can be, well too much. We believe that simplicity is classy too. When you do things in moderation, it shows you know your self-worth and you do not need to prove yourself to anyone. We do not brag about our achievements either.

13. PUNCTUALITY: We know how valuable time is and that is why we try to be punctual when we have appointments. Keep in mind that everyone is as busy as you are, and this will always make you not want to keep someone else waiting.

14. DOING THINGS IN MODERATION: Drinking too much is a sign of self-disrespect. When you drink too much and start to misbehave or get obnoxious, it tells a lot about your being. We're sure you don't want to be remembered for how you act when you drink.

15. TABLE MANNERS: Feminine women eat elegantly. We don't chew noisily or talk with our mouths open. We clean around our mouths often when eating and we eat slowly in bits. No one wants to be left gasping for air because a bone got stuck in her throat.

Importance Of Etiquette Practice

When you treat people with respect, it is also an indirect way of telling them to treat you with respect. They won't have issues doing this because you have shown similar respect to them. It's like a give-and-take exchange. You can't get what you don't give. Etiquette practices are self-development methods that build your character and relationship with people. It also creates an excellent reputation for you. People see you as a person of value and this attracts them to you. Setting healthy values and respectfully disagreeing when necessary are only a few ways to achieve this. Because we value ourselves and we don't have to be aggressive to prove a point.

Try practicing these feminine etiquettes and see how your femininity will be strengthened. Implementing them in your daily lifestyle will help you get used to them and you can always improve with practice. You don't have to follow all the etiquette practices mentioned in this mentioned, you can create your etiquette practices too!

12

THE FEMININE QUALITIES THAT IT GIRLS POSSESS

Femininity Is Intrinsic To Being An IT Girl.

Your femininity is an enchanting quality that lets you be you! As IT Girls, using our feminine qualities has helped us build healthier relationships with people. It has helped us to see the beauty of being feminine. Little wonder how many people find us charming. Feminine power is an intrinsic quality that we all have, but the difference lies in how we harness such an important element in our lives.

You might wonder how to tap into this feminine power you never knew existed in you naturally. No need to worry! Let's talk about it.

You can only know how to tap into your feminine qualities if you know what feminine qualities are. To us, there is no better definition of feminine qualities than that which says that feminine qualities are those attributes that make us who we truly are.

Ten Female Qualities That IT Girls Possess

Feminine energy is a powerful tool that helps us to get what we want. It is that innate power within us that lets us stay true to ourselves. Most women suppress their feminine energy because they feel they might not be taken seriously or they might be considered weak but what they fail to realize is how to use this for their advantage. There is a lot you stand to gain by simply utilizing your feminine power. Here are ten female qualities that IT Girls possess.

1. EMPATHY: Sometimes we might be mistaken for being too weak while we are being empathic, but this doesn't stop us IT Girls from being true to ourselves. What many people fail to understand is that empathy, as a feminine quality, helps one to deeply connect with others. Being

empathic shows that you understand people and this attracts people to you. When you are about others, people would want to be around you. This fosters healthy relationships and builds trust, too.

2. TRUST OF INTUITION: IT Girls pay attention not only to their emotions but to the emotions of others and what goes on around them. Our intuition is like a superpower that allows us to naturally feel things sometimes. You need to listen to your inner self and learn to use these magical powers of yours to your advantage.

3. COLLABORATION: Being overly independent can make you unconsciously want to always do things on your own with no help from others. Having that team spirit and working together with others is an even better way to do things. When we work together with people, we support and encourage them. It is our unselfish way of not wanting to succeed alone but also involving others in our success journeys as well.

4. HUMILITY: Be careful not to mistake humility for self-deprecation. Being humble is a way of realizing that you don't have or know it all. Being humble has made us have open minds towards things. It also gives room for us to admit that we can be wrong sometimes and it helps us to willingly accept corrections when necessary.

5. VULNERABILITY: This, as well as empathy, are often mistaken for weaknesses. Being vulnerable doesn't make you weak rather, it lets people see you for who you truly are. It makes you the human you are; imperfect, flawed, and fallible. Although we may seem to always be in control of what goes on in our lives, it doesn't stop us IT Girls from being vulnerable. We understand that sometimes you may feel that when you are vulnerable people might not respect you anymore, but people are attracted to vulnerable people. Other people see such being vulnerable as being authentic.

6. SELF-AWARENESS: When you know whom you are by defining your values, boundaries, strengths, passion, and style, you know how best to help others, too. Style doesn't only mean outfits and dressings. This can be your way of doing things. Even the way you flash that smile of yours. IT Girls are elegant ladies that know the value attached to being pretty and polished. We exude these qualities in our everyday lives and that makes us very attractive.

7. BEING FLEXIBLE: Being rigid helps no one. Sometimes, it makes you closed-minded and you don't want to try out new things. Be spontaneous and open-minded. It saves you the stress of overthinking things most time.

8. WELL-ORGANIZED: IT Girls always seem to be there right on time. Our secret to this is that we are well-organized and we plan ahead of time.

9. EXPRESSIVENESS: We are bold enough to convey our thoughts and feelings effectively. Expressing yourself can come through creativity. Learn to let that creative side of you flow unrestrained. Sometimes, we give the best at the least expected moments.

10. BEAUTY: Beauty is not just physical but also emotional. All the above-listed feminine qualities and several others, make you truly beautiful.

Giving off feminine energy comes with peace because you are simply being you! You are happier and interact well with others. It makes you more confident and you establish healthier and better relationships with people. Now is the time to become intentional when tapping into your feminine qualities. To be that irresistible IT Girl, learn to embrace and own your feminine qualities.

Choosing To Be Soft

A big part of being feminine is being soft. Nowadays being soft has been seen as being weak and meek and we're telling you that couldn't be further from the truth. Being soft means having a soft demeanor that creates tranquility and peace. Softness is connected with your feminine essence. Being soft is being warm, tender, harmonious, and gentle. Being soft gives you the chance to authentically connect with yourself. It's through your softness with yourself and others you can be guided to finding your life purpose and not feel lost and overwhelmed but be led with direction and confidence in who you are. Through vulnerability, you create the space for comfort not only for yourself but for others around you to be just as open. Being vulnerable allows you to build authentic relationships rather than the separation that being hard can create. So in choosing to be your natural feminine self you gain strength just by being soft. Not only do you have the ability to cultivate community and strengthen your community through it, but you also invite others around you to feel safe and to let their guard down. People can feel and see your softness and become less defensive around you. So when deciding to lean into your femininity know that being soft is a strength that can direct you into spaces that being hard just won't allow.

13

HOW TO MAKE OTHERS DROOL AND STUTTER AROUND YOU

One of the things that IT Girls naturally do is have people fawning all over them. Being admired and loved while trying to figure ourselves out is just a byproduct of being as amazing as you see yourself to be. You are the IT Girl and to get someone's attention you must remember that everything is first visual. So we'll start with how you look. The goal is to always look your best. Always be dressed for the occasion and if you do not know what the occasion is then overdress. Yes, we said it. Overdress for the occasion if you aren't sure how to dress but of course, be mindful. You wouldn't want to go on a surprise date wearing a wedding dress. But always be polished and wear clothes that compliment your body. Be sure that you look and feel confident and always add a smile. When it comes to physical appearances, be sure that your style looks effortlessly put together. We mean you are wearing the dress and that the dress is not wearing you. Your hairstyle should compliment your look. Your makeup should be part of your signature style. This may seem like rules and lots of them, but the point here is when someone, or we'll say anyone sees you, they should be able to see you and not just the composition of you. It should look like natural glam regardless of what you are wearing. When you hear women say 'this old thing' knowing good and well they look stunning in it...the people that are complimenting them are complimenting them on how natural they look with what they are wearing. So anytime someone sees you, their memory of you should always make them say she always looks amazing and there is something about her. Each time someone sees you they will be in awe of how you always look effortless and how you inspire them to also look their best. It will always be part of the story they tell about you in their mind and what they tell others about how you look like everything works out in your favor.

Remember that being 'droolable' it's because of your charisma. Being a very optimistic person with self-confidence, you do not bash others. You do not complain. You have ambitions, you are lovable, you are magnetic, you are friendly and you look at the bright side of things (again optimistic). Did we mention that you have other things going on for yourself while looking amazing? This is how you make others drool and stutter over you. You do this by being your dream self that encompasses all of these traits and more. You have so many people waiting to love you and be around you when you step into the IT Girl we know that you are. You become simply magnetic to the best in life, and everyone who experiences a moment with you will never forget it because they are enamored with you. When they are in your view all they do is stare while trying to get themselves together because of the work you put towards working on your self-confidence.

Another thing to remember is to never show anyone your struggles or anything you may be stressing out about. This doesn't mean you are not allowed to have feelings or be able to consult with anyone. It means when you are out in public you only show your best face. You can put everything to the side and be happy and present at the moment because you know your presence influences others. If you find it hard to show your best face for an event or anything you are invited to then do not attend. Being an IT Girl means you influence those around you and it's important to recognize that you are always being watched. When you are seen in a calm, happy, confident state you always catch eyes looking at you wanting to know more. You may have individuals come up to you at this point just to want to talk or even stand next to you to be by you to see up close just how amazing you are. If you are approached by someone and a conversation is initiated by the individual always look the person in the eye, then ask the person for their name, and always address them by their name. Whatever the conversation is about always be sure to ask that person questions about themselves while keeping the conversation short and friendly and genuine to you. By just acknowledging the individual by name, directing questions to them while being friendly and keeping it short you have just created an amazing experience for that person who when they will see you will always be in admiration with how you carry yourself, how you style yourself and how special you made them feel. Everything is based on how you made someone feel and if they feel like they had an amazing experience with you they will always be your biggest cheerleader whenever and if ever they see you because you are just that influential.

14

BECOMING INFLUENTIAL

The thing about being an IT Girl who is influential is that it is not something that happens in just a day. To outsiders, you appear influential because of the type of people you attract around you as you work on yourself and start to exude a more powerful, feminine, graceful, and confident demeanor. But it's more than just what it looks like. It is what you actually are. When it comes to being an influential IT Girl, you must recognize the following....

- IT Girls Know How To Cultivate Relationships To Build A Strong Network
- Understand Their Star Quality
- Create Their Path To Success
- Have The Ability To Adapt To Any Situation And Shine In Their Skin
- Knows How To Be The Center Of Attention
- Has The Emotional Intelligent To Manage Stress
- Willing To Take Risk
- Always Expanding Her Skills And Knowledge
- She's About Intentional Action
- Engages In Healthy Habits
- Has Mental Strength
- Doesn't Shrink Herself For Other People's Comfort Or To Fit Other People's Standards

IT Girls Know How To Cultivate Relationships To Build A Strong Network

So the first thing you must know how to do is to build a team. What does that mean? Well, just that. A strong reliable team could look like anything in your world. This can be if you are starting a business making sure you are creating a team that you can rely on to get things done. An IT Girl knows how to do this through conversation and skill as well as knows how to put other people together to help each other out and build an even stronger network. Whatever you need to get done, you most likely will know an IT Girl who knows or has access to someone wonderful to get the job done amazingly well. Whether your team is a glam team, tech team, personal trainer, yoga instructor, or banker...these are all people that you may have personal connections with as well as professional connections.

Understanding Your Star Quality

Oh you know you are a star and we know this about you too. That's why you are reading this. There is so much more to you. You are compelling in the most organic way. You can draw people's attention to you, win trust in seconds, and have a great presence. When someone sees you they know you are IT Girl and hold you in the highest regard in the word. Having star quality is not simply about being a celebrity or having social status. When you have star quality, it is just not something you can hide. People recognize it and want to be around it. So when you understand your star power then you start doing things that IT Girls with star quality do, and one of the main things that IT Girls do is bet big on themselves. They learn to accept the fact that they deserve star treatment. You speak with authority (as we love to repeat – due to confidence). You know how to shine when no one is looking and when everybody is watching.

Create Your Path To Success

An influential IT Girl understands that she is the blueprint for her success. Even when there may not seem like there isn't an opportunity or the door is closed, she knows that to her the door is never closed. She doesn't allow other people's fears and failures to stop her from pursuing her own goals and being successful. She knows that even when something did not work out for her it is a learning experience and she keeps going. She knows success is bound to happen for her in the way that she defines it. Creating your path to success means knowing that one person's way of doing things does not mean that is the exact way to do it. She knows how to learn from others while following her intuition. It's not all about going the traditional route (unless that works for you). You can break barriers and knock on new doors if needed, to get to your end goal.

Have The Ability To Adapt To Any Situation And Shine In Their Light

When change is inevitable you can either resist the change or choose to adapt to it. IT Girls tend to choose to quickly learn to adapt. There is no use in complaining about the change or the process of it. When it comes to the newness and the newness around the newness, IT Girls see opportunities where others see failure and exercise a huge amount of energy in resisting. The habits and thoughts that have previously created desired results have now changed and IT Girls tend to be the first to shine in the environment of the change that has been created. We think ahead due to the open minds that we exhibit. So what is new to others, we simply embrace mentally, physically, emotionally, and spiritually.

Knows How To Be The Center Of Attention

Well, we are stars. Enjoy the attention when you decide to glow up and change things from the inside and out. But to know how to be the center of attention is quite different. We don't look for attention unless necessary and even then our star quality just brings out our light. We know how to tastefully use our attention to influence in the most positive way. We do not fight for attention and never have to.

Has The Emotional Intelligent To Manage Stress

Being influential does come with a few situations that may be deemed as stressful or even triggering. These situations can cause you to feel irritable, depressed, angered, and more. Learning how to manage your stress as soon as you feel and see the first signs is key. IT Girls know what they need to do for themselves to balance their lives and deal with the stress that may cause them to not make the best decisions and lose their ability to focus. This is when she demands more rest for herself, practices meditation seeks a therapist, engages in physical exercise, and simply just steps away to put herself first and deal with any heavy feeling and mental overload that needs to be addressed and relieved from herself. To be influential you must know what you need, when you need it and how to provide it to yourself from within.

Willing To Take Risk

Because we focus on our desires, we are willing to take the risk that can change the lives of ourselves and others. We take educated intuition and spirit-guided risks. We learn from the outcome either way and build to get in a way that gets us closer to our outcome. We take the risk to change the current status and try new things that may lead us towards a new path of creativity, discovery, and more. The risk taken is because we bet on ourselves. We hear the yes within us and know the calculated risk that needs to be taken to fulfill the part of our journey in life. Now influential women take these risks and gain huge rewards that leave them with a great story to tell and in turn lead to others looking up to them.

Always Expanding Her Skills And Knowledge

From whatever she is interested in she is always finding ways to learn more. She invests in herself to expand her knowledge in whatever interest her so that she can be the best and get the desired results she is looking for. If there is a particular talent or skill she has, she spends time perfecting her craft to the best of her ability and continues to put it into use and practice over and over again until it feels right to her. She doesn't get easily disappointed when something doesn't go her way or has to take some time to perfect. She is truly emotionally, financially, and timewise invested in getting better. She works with others who do what she does and can teach her how to improve. If she needs a mentor she will invest in one. She doesn't make excuses for why she is not where she wants to be with her skills. The art of focus and good habits becomes her best friend. She believes in herself and those around her are influenced by her ability to focus and become great at whatever she wants to do.

She's About Deliberate Action

IT Girls know when to make moves. We don't use our energy to just do anything and everything. We do not talk just to be talking. We say what we mean and we mean what we say. We stand by our words. We stand by any commitment we make. We can back up anything we say we will do with action and every action we make is intentional. Our actions have a reason for them. There is always a reason for us to act and we do so with a sound mind. We're never forced to act nor pushed to act. We have a plan to win, inspire and connect. We don't make false promises and talk just to join the crowd. You can forget gossip because we do not engage in that. Most of the time we are the ones being gossiped about because many are trying to make up something about us when they can't figure us out.

We don't make immediate moves unless necessary. We know how to observe what is going on around us and evaluate the best action to take for the overall picture. It's not an emotional act that is taken with us. We're influential because of the deliberate actions we take to reach certain goals for ourselves.

Engages In Healthy Habits

You can always count on IT Girls to indulge in healthy habits because we know the results that come from it. Some of the healthy habits that we do practice are exercising, having daily 'me' time, drinking water, eating healthy, having a morning and night time routine and so much more. Now from time to time we may steer off and eat something that may not be healthy like not taking our makeup off before bed because we are just so tired. But we are also balanced women who make our own rules and enjoy life. We engage in healthy habits because we know what kind of life we want and healthy habits help us to get there as a whole person. What we mean by whole we mean mentally, emotionally, spiritually, and physically. We take our healthy habits seriously because we love how it makes us feel and the results we get from them. Influential IT Girls create and maintain healthy habits for a happier, healthier, and easier life ahead. We can identify unhealthy habits, make an action plan towards that unhealthy habit to change it into a positive one, and then execute while creating benchmarks for growth and improvement. We are patient when it comes to creating a healthy habit. We know that by creating a healthy habit, you do not have to do anything with the unhealthy habit as that is no longer the focus and is currently being replaced with this new habit.

Has Mental Strength

Mental strength is something that is built for many over time. Having the ability to effectively deal with challenges and things and/or environments that causes pressure and still perform at your best is having mental strength. Being able to break past unhealthy habits and still do what is best for you is mental strength. IT Girls know how to be present in the moment and embrace adversity. We aren't defeated by fear and are aware of how we talk to ourselves. We don't go in the direction of the crowd when we know that another direction is better for ourselves and everyone around us as a whole. In times when we may feel like we are defeated we know how to get back up and continue to push ourselves. We are resilient. IT Girls know how to not let noise influence our decisions and to be able to hear themselves and continue to make the decisions that they can be proud of. IT Girls with mental strength know the power of repetition. We know how to build mental strength by telling ourselves positive affirmations over and over again to build our belief within ourselves. When you have others who may try to tear you down or have you question who you are and what you do; your mental strength, spiritual strength, as well as your emotional strength, will help protect you from having other people's opinions and thoughts affect you.

Doesn't Shrink Herself For Other People's Comfort Or To Fit Other People's Standards

IT Girls do not shrink. We expand. We do not shrink or try to become digestible for other people to be able to understand us or relate to us. The goal for us was never to meet other people's standards but to create, live and meet our standards for ourselves. We know we are what we can control and do not change what we do for the sake of making others happy when it doesn't make us happy and does some long-term damage. We are influential because we elevate others to be better because of how we choose to live our lives. We do not worry about if others like us because we know we are everybody's type. Those who do not like us for the most part (if they have no valid reason) choose not to like us because they have their insecurities that they need to deal with (

← This is not intended to be a gaslighting statement. This is to shed light on the truth of people who do not like you but never even met you and have chosen not to like you). We stand strong and who we are and whom we have chosen to be and continue to influence others because of how different we are inside and out and love ourselves and others for who they are as well.

Be fully aware that in your becoming an IT Girl, your influence is important and comes with the decisions you choose to make. You will thrive and the characteristics of an IT Girl that makes a difference have been listed so you can see within yourself whom you are becoming and what we know you already are.

15

LET'S TALK HYGIENE

Having a good personal hygiene regimen is extremely important when it comes to defining yourself as an IT Girl. Being able to keep all parts of your external body clean and healthy is important in both maintaining proper physical and mental health. We do not only work on our inner being but also on our physical bodies that help us grow our self-confidence and keep us healthy. Hygiene can cover many areas but we are focusing on the areas of cleanliness. So what this means is truly loving yourself in a space where you recognize the importance of being clean and keeping up with yourself on a regular schedule to always make sure you are at your best optimal health with all parts of your body.

What does having good personal hygiene look like? Well, this looks like:

- MAKING SURE YOU CLEAN YOUR BODY DAILY – this means taking showers daily. Use a washcloth to apply a bar of soap to your body and rinse. But don't just stop there. To not only be clean but to smell extra good and be moisturized, use a moisturizing body wash and apply it to a loofah and rub from the shoulders down to the length of your body not forgetting areas like your back and in between your toes. From time to time use a body scrub to exfoliate your skin and body oil to lock in moisture after a shower.

- MAKING SURE YOU BRUSH YOUR TEETH AND TONGUE TWICE A DAY, FLOSS, AND USE MOUTHWASH – You may be saying to yourself doesn't everyone do this? And the answer is no. Besides obvious dental hygiene reasons, it's important to keep your mouth clean as you want to always have great-smelling breath. The buildup of bacteria in your mouth will cause bad breath amongst other things like cavities and gum disease. We recommend using an electronic toothbrush to reach places you may not be realizing your missing as well as flossing before brushing your teeth. Use a mouthwash to help prevent cavities and plaque buildup while having a fresh breath. Mouthwash should not be used in replacement of brushing your teeth and flossing. It's great to carry a travel size with you after having a quick lunch or a dinner date.

- MAKING SURE YOU WASH YOUR HANDS WITH SOAP AFTER USING THE TOILET – Each time you use the toilet wash your hands with soap. It doesn't matter if you did or did not touch anything (we strongly have to put this out there). Always wash your hands. Hand sanitizer can only do so much and does not replace actual soap and water. Use a moisturizing soap if possible to wash your hands and be sure to follow up with a hand moisturizer to infuse more moisture and soften your hands. Also, we should add that keeping your nails clean is part of keeping your hands clean. Making sure to remove any trapped dirt under and around your nails to ensure the healthy growth of your nails is crucial.

- MAKING SURE YOU WASH YOUR FACE TWICE A DAY OR MORE DAILY AND KEEPING IT moisturize – Washing your face two times or more is extremely important to remove dirt, sweat, and impurities that cannot be seen. While this is part of having a great skincare routine, making sure your face is clean allows the skin to breathe while helping it to stay younger-looking. Always evaluate what the skin on your face needs by determining if you have oily, dry, or combination skin and treating your facial skin based on that. Don't just stop with your face, cleaning your neck and especially your ears are also important to remember. When it comes to your ears you can go to a doctor to ask to get any ear wax removed or if you choose you can use an ear wax softener to soften earwax for easier removal. Be sure to use a damp washcloth or cotton swab to clean the outside of your ear without entering into your ear canal. It's always important to make sure your face is clean as much as possible. When you hear the term 'having a fresh face,' this means a clean-looking face. IT Girls love this look!

- MAKING SURE THAT DURING THE TIMES YOU ARE MENSTRUATING YOU ARE CHANGING YOUR PAD/TAMPON SEVERAL TIMES A DAY – For obvious reasons other than feminine hygiene, changing your pad/tampon is not only important for sanitary reasons but crucial in the development of bacteria in your private area that can grow and cause other vaginal conditions. An unclean vaginal area can cause odors which of course is not something you as an IT Girl want to be associated with. If you find that you do experience unpleasant strong odors despite the number of times you clean your vaginal area and change your pad/tampon, then consult with a gynecologist as it can be a deeper underlying issue that may be causing this. We do not recommend ever inserting soaps or other unnatural products into the vagina. Daily cleaning of your private area consists of outside cleaning of this area and in between the lips with plain unperfumed soap and water with your hands or a clean washcloth. Also, be sure to keep a clean diet and wear the right panties to help balance your PH levels. Avoid putting anything inside your vagina. For more detailed instructions if needed on cleaning this area, we suggest consulting with your gynecologist to fit your needs.

- MAKING SURE TO TAKE CARE OF YOUR FEET – Feet tends to be one of the most highly neglected areas of our body when it comes to hygiene. No one wants stinky, dry, hard, peeling, and/or itchy feet. Always be sure to clean your feet with warm water and mild moisturizing soap. Be sure to remember to clean in between your toes and to thoroughly dry your feet and in between your toes (as keeping feet somewhat wet can be a breeding ground for bacteria and cause problems such as athletes' foot).

- MAKING SURE YOU USE DEODORANT DAILY – If you do not naturally smell like strawberries and pomegranates then you will want to use deodorant daily (especially in the summer months). Deodorant keeps bacteria away. Deodorants reduce the amount of sweat on the body and works by killing the bacteria on your skin while eliminating the chances of allergies. Smelling fresh is part of having great hygiene and it mentally helps you to feel fresh.

- MAKING SURE THAT YOU PROPERLY WIPE YOURSELF AFTER PEEING – We're saying this because it needs to be said that after peeing it is important to properly wipe yourself from front to back. Never pee and pull up (meaning pulling up your panties). By not wiping yourself you are leaving bacteria on your panties that will cause a foul smell as well as lead to vaginal problems such as UTIs. If needed always carry fresh wipes with you to keep your vaginal area clean and fresh. We do not want any marks or stains in our panties if they can be prevented by simply practicing good hygiene.

Practicing good hygiene keeps us feeling our best, operating at our best, and gives us an overall feeling of confidence. Smelling good plays a huge part in how you feel about yourself. It arouses desirable senses in those that you attract around you as well. Great hygiene is a form of self-love and self-respect.

Taking Care Of Your Hair

How you love your hair is the way it will love you back. Having a great hair care routine that compliments your strands is a form of hygiene that covers how you keep your hair clean, healthy, and attractive. Because we care about our appearance in an effortless manner, we believe hair care is important. When caring for your hair you should know what your hair type is, what your hair needs, and be familiar with the condition of your scalp. Once you know what your hair type is (ranging from 1A, 1B, 1C to 4A, 4B, 4C...from straight to curly to coily) and the condition of your scalp you can start caring for it properly. You'll need to assess if you are experiencing breakage, hair loss, dryness, frizziness, dandruff, hair thinning, or anything else not listed. From here you can start to care for your hair by getting the right cleansing shampoo, conditioner, and necessary leave-ins and oils for your hair. You may from time to time need to incorporate protein treatments and hair masks depending on the condition of your hair during certain seasons. But it doesn't stop there. How you dry your hair and style your hair is also part of your hair care routine if you have any type of healthy hair goal.

CLEANSING: Remember that when cleansing your hair, the goal is to clean the scalp so you can get rid of any product build-up that would clog up your scalp pores. The focus should always be on your scalp as the shampoo will naturally clean the hair strands once it goes down the hair shaft. Be sure when using a hydrating shampoo to possibly cleanse more than once to get rid of buildup and help the shampoo penetrate the scalp. Depending on how much product you put in your hair and how often you apply other products, how often you wash your hair depends on you. We do recommend for individuals with oily scalps to wash two to three times a week and for those with drier scalps to cleanse the scalp with a hydrating shampoo once a week to every two weeks. Cleansing should also depend on things like climate, humidity, sweat, and so forth. Now cleansing your hair is different from wetting and conditioning your hair. If you have extreme build-up, we recommend using a clarifying shampoo which is somewhat of a stronger shampoo that cleans the scalp thoroughly and removes all forms of buildup. This is not something to use often and probably should be used once a month if needed. When using a shampoo like this, it is important to infuse moisture back into the hair as a clarifying shampoo can leave the hair feeling stripped from moisture.

CONDITIONING: Always condition your hair after cleansing your hair with a shampoo to restore moisture. Depending on your hair type, you may or may not need to be heavy-handed with your conditioner. Knowing your hair porosity will also help in knowing how your hair absorbs moisture and if using heat for the conditioner to penetrate the hair is of better advantage to you rather than letting the conditioner just sit on the hair.

MOISTURIZING YOUR HAIR AFTER CONDITIONING: Once you are done with the washing and conditioning process, if you have dry hair it is imperative to add a product that will further hydrate the hair like a leave-in conditioner and seal the hair with some sort of sealing oil.

DRYING YOUR HAIR: Choosing which way to dry your hair for healthy hair is important to decide as air drying is best to give your hair a break from the heat and help prevent hair breakage with excessive blow drying. Consider the style you normally like to wear your hair and the best leave-in products, oils, gels, mousse, or any other product you can use to lock in moisture without weighing your hair down that works for you.

STYLING WITH HEAT: When it comes to styling your hair with heating tools like flat irons, curling irons, diffusers, hot combs, and so forth, you will want to be sure to use some kind of thermal protector/heat protectants to protect your hair strands while using the lowest heat setting possible to achieve the look you are going for.

TREATMENTS: Treatments such as a protein treatment is for hair that has been experiencing breakage. Using a protein treatment provides the protein that the hair strand needs as hair is made up of protein and strengthens the hair and smoothes the cuticle. These types of treatments are on a need as bases and are usually recommended for use every 4-6 weeks or when needed. A hair mask is also a form of treatment used to help treat dryness, split ends, and frizz.

HAIRSTYLES: You may love to constantly style your hair with heating tools, braids, hair accessories, and more, and we know for effortless looks effortless styles come into play to fit the look you are going for. Be mindful if you love trying new hairstyles as you do not want to jeopardize the health of your hair. Be sure to use if you can, low manipulation styles where it keeps your hands out of your hair. If you love changing up your hair color or style often, play with the idea of using extensions or wigs before doing these styles on your actual hair. While we do recommend using hair extensions or wigs or tape-ins, please be sure to have the hair look as natural as possible with your hair and scalp (meaning making sure it can easily blend in). It's great to have fun and experiment with hairstyles and chemicals on extensions while keeping your hair safe from the damage that can come from doing this often. Be sure to consult with a professional to keep your hair safe and clean under your extensions and wigs. If you wear locs and braids, be sure to also keep your roots clean, refreshed, and moisturized to keep breakage and knotting away.

When creating your hair care routine, you must determine what you will need to do for your hair and scalp daily (if anything is to be done daily). Some key things we would like to note is to never ignore your hair at night. Sleep with your hair up, in a silk cap, or sleep on a silk pillow to prevent your hair from breaking. Also, be sure to get trims when needed to get rid of split ends. If you are into the straight neat look, a trim would help you to achieve this look. Lightly dusting your hair (this is just cutting less than a trim and only on certain strands when needed) for split ends also helps in having healthy hair. Be sure to be gentle when detangling your hair and always start from the ends moving your way up to your roots. If you have dry hair, be sure to always keep your hair moisturized to keep it from breaking. This could mean moisturizing your hair daily or every other day.

Creating a hair routine that works well for your hair and your hair goals may take some trial and error with figuring out the right products that work well with your hair strands and your hair needs. You may have to decide whether you care to use only natural products, professional salon products, create your own DIY products, etc. The key is the order of how you use your products and the consistency of giving your hair strands the love that it deserves. Shower your scalp by keeping it clean and providing daily five-minute scalp massages for blood circulation. For healthy hair, it all starts from within and with your diet. Protein is important as this is the makeup of your hair strands as well as iron, vitamin A and C, and omega-3 fatty acids. Biotin as well as B7 is also important to grow healthy strong hair strands from root to tip. Be sure to drink lots of water and be mindful of the nutrients your body needs. Love your hair by showing it love and you and others will be able to see the difference.

Taking Care Of Your Skin

Skincare is a holistic practice that involves cleansing, exfoliating, nourishing, and protecting the skin from the sun. Cleansing involves using a foam or gel-based face wash to remove oily pores and dirt stuck in your pores. In the next phase, the skin is exfoliated and gently scrubbed to get rid of whiteheads and blackheads. The third step is nourishing the skin by choosing the right moisturizer and serum and applying a toner to close the pores. Nowadays, serums are becoming increasingly popular as they nourish your skin from 10 layers deep. Finally, apply sunblock to protect yourself from UV rays.

To choose and apply the right skin care products, you must first learn about the types of skin.

There are mostly three types of skin that are commonly found.

1. Dry Skin
2. Oily Skin
3. Combination Skin

To learn more about these types of skin, let's discuss them briefly.

<u>What To Know About Dry Skin</u>

Skin dryness is a condition characterized by scaling, itchiness, and cracking. Various causes can contribute to the dryness of your skin. It may be a natural condition. Even if you have oily skin, sometimes you will experience dry skin.

The condition of having dry skin is also popular as xerosis or xeroderma. This condition of dry skin can happen due to extremely cold environments, harsh products, sun damage, and more. In this condition, the skin looks rough, flaky, and itchy most of the time. Due to the extreme dryness of the skin, the dry skin may also start to peel off and become scaly.

The condition of dry skin happens to people of all ages and is quite common in the teenage age.

To prevent dry skin conditions, we can share a few of our skin secrets with you. Make your skin hydrating and nourishing with these following skin tips, and take care of your skin from within.

1. Apply ample moisturizing creams or moisturizing serums.
2. Use hydrating products that are enriched with essential oils, coconut, and other nourishing ingredients.
3. Consume tons of water and liquids to make your skin look refreshing.

To improve your skin on your own, you can make sure to use sunblock as well as other moisturizing products on the skin.

What To Know About Oily Skin

Similar to having a dry skin condition, the other half of the population suffers from an oily skin condition. If you are tired of wiping your face repeatedly to remove the excess oil from your skin, then we are here for you.

Oily skin is a condition where our skin produces a noticeable amount of oil and makes the skin look oily and greasy. The production of sebum is necessary to maintain healthy skin. Nevertheless, too much sebum can cause oily skin, clogged pores, and acne.

Making regular skin care a habit is often necessary for managing oily skin. It is possible to reduce the amount of oil on the skin by washing regularly. You should avoid soaps containing fragrances, or harsh chemicals, because they can irritate and dry out the skin, making it produce more oil.

When your glands start to produce more sebum than is required to keep the skin nourished, it is said that the skin is oily. In such cases, the skin starts creating a greasy layer on the top which then causes acne and clogged pores.

To care for your oily skin, you must make sure to consume water and provide hydration to your skin. The oily skin can be easily managed with the help of some homemade skin care masks and scrubs.

What To Know About Combination Skin

Another type of skin condition is combination skin which is popularly known as combo skin.

People with combination skin types have dry, flaky cheeks while other areas of the face have excessive oil and shine. The forehead, nose, and chin of those who have combination skin are often in a constant fight with excess sebum production. It is common for those who have combination skin to experience oily shine on some portions of their faces. The T-Zone is the most common area where this shine occurs, and it is caused by excess oil production.

In this type of skin condition, it can get a bit difficult for the person to manage their skin due to extreme dryness and oily areas.
People who have combination skin conditions get easily confused that they should apply moisturizer to balance the dry skin or wipe the excess oils off their skin.

To take care of your combination skin, you must use moisturizer mixed with rose water. The pH level of the rose water will balance out the skin pH, and the moisturizer can work on hydrating the skin.

Managing the combination skin can be easy if you take care of your skin regularly. With continuous care, your skin will start to look ravishing and hydrating in no time.

Creating The Ultimate Skin Care Routine For Your Skin

To take proper and good care of your skin, make sure to follow the below-mentioned skincare routine steps regularly.

Cleanser

The first step in this skincare routine is to use a cleanser (organic cleanser preferably). Make sure to use a natural ingredient-based cleanser on an everyday basis. Clean your skin and remove all the dirt. If you have oily skin, try to use a foam-based cleanser to clean the dirt from the inside of the skin. Whereas if you have dry skin, you should use a gel-based or cream-based cleanser. Now pat your skin dry and move to the next step.

Toner

The next step that you must follow to take care of your skin is to apply toner. A toner can help you improve your skin's texture and make your skin look radiant.

Antioxidant Serum

Another step in your skincare routine is using hydrating serums. This step is necessary only for dry skin types. The oily skin types can skip this step. Applying serum to your skin will add an additional layer of hydration to the skin and will help in improving the texture of your skin. Serums help in healing the skin and make it look spotless.

Eye Cream

Including an eye cream in your skincare routine is as important as any other step. Using an eye cream under your eyes is the best way to keep those dark circles at bay. Eye creams help moisturize the under-eye area and prevent it from darkening due to dehydration.

Using an eye cream that is enriched with vitamin B3 can work wonders for your under eyes as vitamin B3 is best for brightening your skin and helps in eliminating hyperpigmentation. Applying eye cream every day will also help in reducing puffiness from your eyes, making them beautiful.

Moisturizer

While choosing a moisturizer, you must make sure to select a moisturizer as per your skin condition. If you have oily skin, we suggest you purchase a gel-based moisturizer that will make your skin hydrating but won't make it greasy. Whereas if you have dry skin, then the perfect moisturizer for you to keep your skin hydrated is creamy-based moisturizers.

A cream-based moisturizer will help to penetrate the hydration deep in your skin and make it look youthful and fresh.

Sunblock

The last but most necessary step that no skin type must skip is to apply a layer of protection from the UV rays. Make sure to apply tons of sunblock and protect your skin from the conditions of early aging, dark spots, hyperpigmentation, and acne.

The importance of good skin care goes beyond your appearance. The skin is the largest organ in your body, so it is crucial for your overall health. Thus, it is imperative to have a well-planned skin care regimen. Taking care of your skin daily is worth your time and effort and is just part of being an IT Girl.

Taking Care Of Your Nails

Your fingernails and toenails are there to protect the inner layer of skin underneath the tip of your fingers and toes. Taking good care of your nails on each part of your body is part of having good hygiene. The ideal condition of fingernails and toenails is for them to be strong, smooth, and healthy looking. They do not have any spots or discoloration. Keeping your nails a good desirable workable length that would free them from getting ripped, torn, and split is a great ground for developing a good nail care routine. Many times it is easier to go to a professional who can pamper your nails and address any issues you may have, but if time and convenience are something that prevents you from seeing a professional regularly, then implementing a good nail routine can help you to transform weak damaged nails to strong healthy nails in a short amount of time. A healthy nail care routine consists of:

- Keeping Your Nails At A Desirable Workable Length And Trimming Your Nails When Needed
- Practicing The Habit Of Not Biting Your Fingernails Or Picking At Your Nail Cuticles
- Using A Moisturizer Not Only On Your Hands But On Your Fingernails And Cuticles As Well
- Clipping Off Hangnails

- Removing Dirt Daily From Underneath Your Nails By Washing Your Hands Repeatedly
- Using A Nail Hardener To Help Strengthen Nails
- Staying Away From Cheap Nail Polish That May Cause Your Nails To Turn Yellow
- Taking Daily Supplements Such As Biotin That Can Help Strengthen Your Nails And Fix Brittle Fingers.

While we know we IT Girls love nail designs and nails at a variety of lengths, taking care of the nails underneath the use of acrylics, gels and dips is important. Realize that if you notice spots, white lines, and tints of yellow happening on your nails and this is not due to cheap nail polish, you should consult with your dermatologist as your nails can indicate a much deeper rooted issue with your health.

Your nails on both your fingers and toes can help boost your self-confidence and is an act of self-love when taken care of. You don't ever have to feel self-conscious about not taking care of your nails. Spending a lot of money on your nails doesn't necessarily mean you are taking care of your nails in the best way. We want you to know even your DIYS can give you a proud feeling of being able to take care of yourself while making yourself look and feel nice. Splurge on that nail design or keep it simple and clear, you decide. But whatever you choose, keep it clean, dirt free, and polished.

16

CREATING YOUR
SIGNATURE STYLE
UNIQUE STYLE IDENTITY

So this is where all IT Girls have fun and that is in dressing up. We do it with such ease. We tend to know what look we want to convey and just pull it off so effortlessly. Sidenote: if you haven't already figured it out, our keyword when it comes to describing IT Girls is effortless. We can pull anything off because we have the confidence to do so. If you are trying to establish a signature style or create a new unique style identity regardless of where you are in life, know that you can easily do so by simply taking a look at the lifestyle you currently hold and whom you are wanting to become as an IT Girl. So let's get into actually creating a signature style or signature look.

A signature look is a few elements that at its core becomes your style. When people see a certain look they will automatically attribute that look to you. Whether it be in clothes or makeup, it can be somewhat of a guarantee that you will have a look that can easily be identified to you. Whether you want to be known as someone who always wears white, is always seen in a blazer, or is someone who only wears form-fitted dresses, your signature look is something many will always identify you by. But as IT Girls, that is not enough. You do not just want to be identified by a certain look. You want to be identified as being one of the very few who can pull off the look without effort. You want to know you look amazing. You want to be the muse for others who want to adopt a similar look because of how you wear it. So when developing your signature style we say find a muse. Yes, you are a muse to others but you will also want to find one or two individuals who are a muse to you. Think of an era where you loved the clothing and the way things were styled. Look at the jewelry that was paired with those styles as well as the hairstyles and makeup. Once you find the muse, era, and look you are going for, personalize it to fit you. Fitting you means fitting your body and avoiding trendy looks but using basics and incorporating high and low-end items into your look. For example, while everyone may be into jeans and sneakers, why not start playing around with leather skirts and heels with different leather or jean jackets to mix? Now, this might not sound so special but it is in how you wear it. You might bring back the look of chokers and find a more modern way to wear them. You may find that you want to wear vintage designer pieces like a 1949 Dior jacket and a leather Christian Lacroix black skirt that can't easily be duplicated but worn in different ways and fit the look you are going for. Signature pieces for you might be always wearing a jacket in a different way, the choker, the way you do your hair and make-up. It could be just anything but you will of course be remembered for how you wear the outfit (not letting the outfit wear you) and how you look in it.

Another way to narrow in on your signature look is to create a fashion mood board for yourself. This mood board is what you look at to guide you in creating your ideal signature look. On your mood board, you can put the current colors that you are really into, some items you would like to own, and fabrics you like to pair together. Your mood board is a great way to somewhat tell your story in fashion and figure out what direction you would like to head in. This is where you can not only think about what colors compliment you and your look and what you want to be into but also what items you need to accomplish the look. For example, if you're into a very polished look, dark look, or retro glam look, putting this out clearly on your fashion mood board will help you in knowing how to execute the look. So putting items like swatches of patterns, and images of any designers that fit your look and concepts will help you bring your unique style identity to life. This will also help you when shopping for some of your items and aid in the confidence of being able to accomplish the looks you are going for.

When creating a signature style always work with a look that you feel works with your current body type. When you know your body type, it makes it easier to know what will compliment you. Also, you will want to consider your lifestyle. If you are always working out and always wearing workout clothes, think about how you can spruce that up and change up your look while being practical but stylish. Consider colors you haven't worked with before or paired together. Know what patterns compliment you. Play with textures by mixing them and layering them and if you feel like you need to, hire a personal stylist to help you in not only creating looks but by locating hard-to-find pieces.

A Few Tips For Dressing Your Best:

- Be Sure To Invest In Essential Pieces And What You Would Consider Staples – White T-Shirts, Great Fitted Pair Of Jeans...Etc.
- Match Your Accessories With Your Outfit
- Remember That Heels Dress Up Most Outfits
- Mix Up Sophistication With Sexy
- Mix Up Different Layers Of Clothing
- Always Wear Your Size And Not A Size Smaller Where It Looks Too Tight And Makes Marks Into Your Skin

Creating your unique signature style doesn't have to be a challenge. We find this fun. We say work with what you have. Decide what features you want to always accentuate. That can be your legs, hips, curves, eyes, lips, and so on, and learn how to curve your style to compliment these features while creating looks that you can make your own and evolve with. When you start to know what works well for you, in due time you will be able to easily put together looks that look made just for you with no effort.

Selecting Your Luxury Designer Style

We love luxury. Yes, we do. Our name is called IT Girl Luxury. Everything we want we want it to be luxurious. From luxurious dinners, travel, and overall experiences we want it to be rich in memories and ultimate extravagant living.

Now extravagant living doesn't even mean it can't be simple. Being in a state of great comfort with something so simple can be determined as luxury. But as of right now in this book we are going to talk about luxury fashion and luxury designer style. Luxury fashion is branded as a high level of quality, and exclusivity and typically comes with high price tags. Other elements that define luxury brands are the craftsmanship (and taking pride in that), its rich history of providing quality, the prestigious feeling that comes with the brand/clothing, the ability to last a long time because of its quality, the sophistication of the details and the creativity of the item. We just love luxury! We love it for all of these reasons and if you are into luxury and want to incorporate luxury designer pieces into your wardrobe then you would first want to consider what your luxury designer style is. Who do you gravitate more to in terms of style, collections, and seasons? Is your style a bit loud and creative like Versace or a bit more quiet and polished like Ralph Lauren? Deciding if you are bold with your style, more into classics, lean towards artistic, or just super casual, you will then be able to narrow a luxury designer that then would fit your needs. From there you would want to look into their past collections and see what season you gravitate towards. For example, you may find yourself truly in love with Chanel when Karl Langerfield was the creative director at that time or Chanel's 2022 traveling Metier D'art collection and every Metier D'art collection by Chanel. This is something you would want to know so you can reserve your most loved pieces when certain collections come out and you see a must-have item that you know will be timeless and something you would enjoy having for a lifetime. With luxury most of the time, we consider a lot of the pieces to be investment pieces. This can mean investments because again they are made with high-quality materials that last a long time and/or they can be sold much later at even a higher rate due to not only the materials but the production of the piece and its exclusivity of it as time goes by and production on it stops.

Remember that with luxury pieces, you can mix and match designers and collections that also fit the look that you are going for, and keep a collection of timeless pieces that you can always archive later as memorabilia.

Learning To Accessorize

So accessories can transform any outfit. A day look can easily turn into a night look with the right accessories. Accessorizing is a great way to even help you create your unique style identity as they are what creates the finishing touches to any look. You can work with belts that can help define your waistline and give you a more polished look or a wide belt that can give you a more fashion-forward look (depending on the belt and what it is paired with). You may also want to accessorize your look with some accessories such as hats, gloves, and scarves. It's all about how you style them.

The best way we love to accessorize a look is with jewelry. You can never go wrong with the right kind of jewelry. Whether they are small hoop earrings to bold and large hoop earrings to a nice watch, from statement necklaces to simple layered necklaces, to diamond stud earrings and pearls you can change up a casual look to a semi-polished look with just your jewelry alone. Always consider your staple pieces and how your accessories will go together. We say accessorize to give a minimal look as well as an overall glam. It can work well either way.

Choosing Your Under Garments

We want you to notice that everything we've talked about dealing with IT Girls and you becoming one is feeling great in your skin. Owning who you are and being confident in your declaration of who you are so effortlessly is part of the reason you are an IT Girl. So right before you start to style yourself from head to toe the first articles of fabric that go on your body belong to undergarments. What we're specifically talking about are your bra and panties. It's easy to dismiss the importance of picking out great underwear and bras. You may think no one is going to see them (or maybe someone might) or it simply just isn't important to you. The truth is there really should be more attention towards picking out the right undergarments for your body as this can make you feel sexy and of course confident.

When choosing your bra and underwear the first thing you should consider is your size. Wearing the right bra is extremely important not just for coverage but also for the support and how smooth it will lay on you. Wearing the right size also in your underwear could help you to prevent those unwanted lines that show through from your jeans, dresses, and skirts. For both your underwear and bras you do not want to get sizes that are too small that go into your skin (which can cause bulges) nor do you want to get garments that are too large the slide off and bulk up.

You also want to make sure that you consider the style and shape of your undergarments and which ones work best for you for your everyday wear and special occasions. For example are you more into racerback bras and bikini-cut panties? You'll want to make sure you get undergarments for certain looks like well-fitted dresses, low backless dresses, and even when it's that time of the month for you to feel comfortable. Having a variety that not only looks good but serves its purpose for your daily activities is something to always think about when picking out your undergarments.

Another important factor in picking out undergarments should be the material. Now cotton is the best material for most undergarments because it is very breathable for the skin. Cotton typically works best for everyday use but there may be times when lace, silk, or other materials work better for whatever you choose to wear for the occasion.

We want you to also know that picking two to three places and/or designers that create and/or carry undergarments that you love is a must. The reason for this is due to having consistent sizing, and styles and understanding your needs with the purpose. Your undergarments do not have to be typical or look like everyone else's. Finding places that carry what you like consistently and have sets that you can easily purchase to fit your body type, will save you a lot of time. Having a 'go-to' anything saves a lot of time and always feels catered to you. With undergarments, it should be the same.

Color is also something you must consider. Do you have your basic colors? The essential colors? Having a lot of bright-colored underwear may be fun but they don't work if you only wear neutral color clothing pieces. We suggest always making sure you have basic colors first in every style that you love before expanding into other variations of colors. Basics always seem to be a great go-to when you do not have the other color that you may be wanting to match. So having neon colors in bras and panties before having black, white, neutrals and other skin tone colors wouldn't be something that we advise.

When choosing the right undergarments remember you can never have too much! We don't believe in that. Always choose based on what looks good for your body. Invest in simple matching sets before mixing and matching. Throw away old underwear and bras that are torn, worn out, and have holes in them. Remember to always wear your best undergarments at all times. You always want to be prepared for any occasion that you may have someone else see them.

Undergarments May Include Body Shapers

Undergarments do not just stop at panties and bras. They can also include body shapers. Body shapers are typically used to give the illusion of a much curvier body. They usually are worn to target certain areas on our bodies that we either want to smooth, flatten, make smaller, or bigger. These are undergarments that provide temporary means to reshape the body to your desired look. Here is a breakdown of different types of body shapers.

Waist Cinchers And Tummy Shapers – this type of shapewear helps to define and sculpt your waist. If you're looking to create an hourglass silhouette then using a waist cincher and tummy shaper will help you to achieve that look. These are also good for working out at the gym if you are trying to shape your waist area.

Shaper Shorts – this type of shapewear offers a high waistline that smooths and shapes the waist and tummy area. These types of shorts extend downward and provide thigh slimming support.

Slimming Arm Shapers – this type of shapewear is meant to target your arms and slim sagging regions of your arms. They can help in making your arms appear more toned while reducing any extra jiggle you may have.

Cami Shapers – this type of shaper is made to target the upper torso area. With these shapers, they are great for slimming your tummy and waist area while some may even smooth underarm spillage while providing you with bust support and possibly help you to improve your posture.

Butt And Hip Shapers – this type of shaper is designed to cover your hips and smooth your tummy area. When wearing these you can expect a much more defined shape to your hip and butt area. If you're looking for a more rounder and well-defined butt that sticks out a bit more, a butt shaper is perfect for achieving this look.

Seamless Shapewear – this is a type of shapewear that compresses certain areas and accentuates and smooths your body. When wearing this type of shapewear you can be comfortable knowing that it won't reveal seams and panty lines. So if you are looking for invisible panties, butt lifters, body suits, and more, then seamless shapewear is what you would want to look for as it comes in many styles and with different levels of support.

Contour Bras – this type of shapewear gives your bust a more unified shapely look. They will support your bust throughout the day while providing posture and back support. This type of shapewear is perfect for those who want to shape their upper back a bit and their underarms while having their bust look more in place.

Shaping Bodysuits – this type of shapewear is great for creating a slimmer silhouette. This shapewear provides full coverage from your upper back and bust to your lower bottom area. Using a bodysuit shapewear, you eliminate the bunching that may occur underneath the bra and towards the top of the briefs.

Control Leggings – this type of shapewear helps to define and shape your legs. It can help sculpt your curves while smoothing out any cellulite. It may also provide support for your tummy and thighs.

Post-Pregnancy Shapewear – this type of shapewear is designed for moms to help flatten areas like the stomach to help achieve their pre-pregnancy figure. Using this shapewear also helps encourage blood circulation while helping to heal abdominal separations as well as incisions from cesarean sections.

While there are many different types of shapewear, you can find one that will help you achieve your goals and target certain areas. This is only one of many options in creating your look. Many women do not wear shapewear and that is also okay. We believe shapewear is a personal choice and if it helps you to achieve the look that you desire then go for it.

Learning Which Shoes Compliment Your Feet And Look

Shoes make a huge fashion statement. They can make or kill a look. Of course, having nicely polished toes also help to make any open-toe shoe look great for you as well regardless of how nice the shoe may be. We wanted to guide you on our recommendations for your foot type and body type. Of course, these are just recommendations and more guidance towards the type of heel we suggest. If you suffer from any type of foot problem then choosing the right shape of a shoe can make a big difference. Remember that the more narrow the heel is and the higher it is the more of your body weight is forced forward onto the ball of your foot.

1. If Your Foot Type Is A Thin Heel, Then We Recommend Ankle Strap Heels.

2. If Your Foot Type Is More Of A High Arch We Recommend A Heel With Arch Support. A Mid-High Heel With Curved In Arch Or Block Heel For Stability.

3. If Your Foot Type Is More Of A Wide Foot, We Recommend Round Toe Or Pointed Toe With A Gradual Point And Wide Fit

4. If You Are Flat Footed, Then We Recommend A Wide Toe Box Heel With Arch Support And Low To Middle Height

So Let's Break It Down By Body Type

PEAR SHAPED BODY TYPE: This type of body shape is identified as those with small busts, tiny waists, and full bottom areas. This body shape tends to have larger legs and wider ankles. Heels like open-toe wedges add length and the bulky style helps balance out the curvier upper body. Also for boots, pointed-toe knee-high and thigh-high boots will do the trick. Slender heels will compliment the legs of those with this body type.

INVERTED TRIANGLE BODY TYPE: This type of body shape is identified as those with a broad chest, wider shoulders, thin legs, and narrow hips. Wearing ankle-strap shoes of any length or size, platforms, wedges, flats, and chunky heels would work. Bold color shoes will work.

HOURGLASS BODY TYPE: This type of body shape is identified as having a tiny accentuated waistline and being very curvaceous in the bust. To elongate and compliment your legs, choose pumps of medium height and pointed toes heels. You can go higher than medium as well. It is best to avoid clunky oversized shoes.

APPLE BODY TYPE: This type of body shape is identified as bulkier in the abdominal area with slim arms and legs with a small bust. The best heels for this body type are stilettos. This will bring attention to your legs. Also, shoes with an ankle strap look amazing with this body type.

SQUARE BODY TYPE: This type of body shape is identified as equal bust, waist, and hip with minimal to no curves. The classic pumps, round-toe shoes, and even loafers work for this body type. These types of heels will elongate your frame.

IF YOU ARE PETITE: For smaller tiny frames, higher heels and pointed toes help to elongate your frame. Stilettos will look amazing on you. Sneakers with thick soles also look great on you.

IF YOU ARE TALL: For taller women, we recommend flat sandals, ballet flats, rounded toes, and peep toes to look cuter and smaller if that is the look you are going for. If you want to wear heels please note that heels will make you look taller but also look amazing on you.

After exploring the type of shoes per foot type and body type, please note that you should choose shoes that compliment and accentuate what you want to be featured. If you are not used to wearing heels then start with wearing lower heels first and work your way up to your comfort. It's up to you whether you choose to prioritize your comfort for style or view style as worthy of temporary discomfort.

We know that having good quality reliable shoes are important and it feels good.

The Bag Types And The Must Haves
In Your Handbags

When talking about accessories you can't forget the bag. From everyday wear to night wear let's explore some fashion bag options that you can use to create your unique style.

THE CROSSBODY BAG – this bag is named for the way it's worn and is perfect for everyday wear as it allows you to keep your hands free while carrying your essentials. These bags sometimes known as sling bags are great for everyday use and are comfortable, stylish, and all-around functional for running errands, shopping, and anything else you can think of. These types of bags come in all sizes. This type of bag can be worn day and night and come in all shapes, styles, colors, and textiles.

THE CLUTCH BAG – this bag can be worn day or night and is simply classy and exude sophistication. They come in many different sizes and colors. Some clutches come with different compartments while others may not. They can come in extravagant styles and even low-key designs. They range from extra-large to extra small bags.

THE MINAUDIERE BAG – this bag is more of a clutch encrusted bag with colored stones, gems, and pearls and is perfect for special events such as weddings, cocktail parties, or any other special event you can think of. This is best used as an evening bag.

THE HOBO BAG – this bag is typically a crescent shape shoulder bag that can be casual for everyday wear. It is usually large and even slouchy and great for traveling and an evening out. It looks and feels stylish without having to do much.

THE SHOULDER BAG – this bag is exactly the name it states. It's a slung-over-shoulder bag. It is functional and one of the most popular bags that are ideal for every day.

THE SATCHEL BAG – this bag usually comes in a medium-large size with short handles. It is quite sturdy and can hold much larger items like laptops and magazines. It's perfect for any working woman's look.

THE TOTE BAG – this bag may be a top contender with the shoulder bag and crossbody bag as a popular bag. It is a large sometimes single-compartment bag that you can keep a lot of items in. It's usually constructed in fabrics such as nylon or canvas but can come in many other materials and is a sophisticated option for carrying large items around daily.

THE BACKPACK PURSE – this bag is mainly thought to be a bag for students but can be used for by many others for traveling, errands, and so forth. These backpack purses also come in different sizes and styles and can be large enough to fit a laptop and small enough to fit just your wallet.

THE WRISTLET – a wristlet is a wallet worn around your wrist and has enough space to carry what you would carry in a wallet but with a little more room to carry lipstick, a phone, keys, and any other extra stuff while keeping your palms free. This bag is great for errands and even evening runs or events such as concerts and festivals.

THE WALLET – a much smaller type of purse that carries credit cards, money, and any other type of small paper stock information.

What do you keep in your bag? We like to keep things simple and organized and always encourage other IT Girls to do the same. One of the things we recommend is when purchasing a quality bag, purchase the matching set that it would come with such as the wallet and/or phone case to match. By doing so not only do you look well-coordinated but it helps you to identify your belongings as well as be organized. We recommend the same in travel bags. Purchase matching quality luxury bags such as rolling soft duffle bags, trunks, wheeled duffel bags, rolling suitcases, etc.

In keeping it simple we recommend carrying the following items in your handbag:

- Cardholder
- Lip Balm
- Keys
- Hand Sanitizer
- Small Sample Of Your Favorite Perfume

And if room allows for more items to be held we say carry if needed the following:

- Aspirin
- Small Sample Of Moisturizer
- Pad/Tampon
- Some Kind Of Mint Or Sample Mouthwash
- Small Portable Charger If Your Phone Is Always Needing To Be Charged
- Sunglasses

Quality matters and when it comes to quality remember that stitching matters and should be symmetrical and consistent throughout the inside and out and well-constructed so it should be made to last and won't fall apart. Also, a good quality bag may include hardware such as clasps, zippers, and other pieces that you would want to be able to glide with ease and be secure. You would want to make sure that decorative pieces and metals are free from tarnish and chipping. If you have a leather bag you want to make sure it is real leather that will last and not crack or break.

17

MAKEUP

Makeup is truly something that we love to play with. With makeup, you can create the most dramatic looks to the softest looks. You can keep it super simple to enhance certain features or go full-blown artistic vibe. The choice is all up to you and the occasion. You'll find that most IT Girls love to keep it simple for everyday looks and choose to do a no makeup look or play with a little color and keep things to a minimal for daytime wear and transition over to a bit more dramatic like a smokey eye look for evening to night wear. With makeup, this is one of the best ways to create a signature look for yourself. While makeup is a comprehensive topic all on its own we want to cover some essential tips for creating the right look that is universal for any vibe that you are going for. You can't miss with our IT Girl recommendations.

The Correct Order Of Makeup (Our Recommendation For Beginners):

Moisturizer

Primer

Liquid Foundation

Concealer

Bronzer

Blush

Highlighter

Eyeshadow

Eyeliner

Mascara

Lip Gloss

Setting Spray & Powder

The Minimal And Quick Way To Get The Look You Want (Our Recommendation For Beginners):

Moisturizer

Foundation

Bronzer

Mascara

Lipstick/Lip Gloss

Tip #1: If you must wear foundation (you do not have to wear foundation), always wear a foundation that is your shade. This of course should be a no-brainer but it truly doesn't always happen. The best way to find your shade is to find a makeup artist who can steer you towards the right foundation for you. Your makeup artist can lead you to the right brand that has the perfect shade of color foundation for you or even show you how to mix certain colors to get the right foundation for your complexion. You may even have a different color on your forehead from the rest of your face. A great makeup artist can steer you in the direction of how to blend foundation to get full coverage and the right look. Look for a foundation that goes well with your face and what we mean by this is if you have oily skin, stay away from foundations that have a lot of oils. If you have dry skin, stay away from foundations that will dry out your skin. While these can be combatted with what you apply to your face before applying foundation, be sure to get a foundation that works well with your skin type and will not seem to cake up by just sitting on your face. When shopping around for the right foundation color, be sure to leave it on for a few hours when trying a sample. This way you can determine how long it will last, how you look in different lighting with the shade, and so forth. When wearing your foundation do not just apply it to your face. Be sure to apply to your neck as well.

Tip #2: Concealer is a must-have. When looking for a concealer, look for one that you can apply under your eye if you have dark circles you would like to conceal as well as other areas of your face that you would like to add a little bit of dimension towards. The key spots for illuminating purposes of concealer are above your cheekbones, the middle of your chin, the center of your forehead, and down the bridge of your nose. Remember that liquid concealers are great if you want light coverage for a large area of your face while stick and compact concealers are better for heavier coverage for more specific areas. We recommend purchasing one concealer that is very similar to your skin tone and works well for coverage of blemishes and another concealer that is a shade lighter than your skin to highlight certain areas of your face. Apply concealer with a damp sponge or makeup brush to create a glowing look while hiding dark under-eye circles.

Tip #3: There are several types of eyeliner. You can choose to use liquid eyeliner, gel eyeliner, and/or pencil eyeliner. We know that eyeliner can take some practice for some if you're not accustomed to applying it. It's like one slip and you have to redo that area all over again. Let's not get started on removing waterproof eyeliner.

If you are a beginner or simply want the ease of applying eyeliner, we recommend using a pencil eyeliner. It's simple to use to create just about any look.

For looks that need a bit more precision, we recommend using a liquid eyeliner. Now while this can get a bit messy you want to be sure not to use too much and to let the liquid dry. Be sure to add short strokes on the lash line and connect the lines where there are gaps with short strokes to get a much more precise look.

For the cat-eye look, you probably want to use gel eyeliner. Liquid eyeliner can be used as well to achieve this look but the gel has comparatively a bit more of an advantage. Gel eyeliners tend to come in a small dish with a thin brush that you can apply similarly to a liquid eyeliner with small short strokes.

Tip #4: Mascara is always a must! We can't emphasize this enough. A good mascara and lip color are enough to complete a look. That's how vital we believe mascara is. There are mascaras for just about every look you are trying to conceive. For thick lashes, voluminous lashes, or long lashes....you can find the right mascara to do all of that and more. We like to use mascaras that we can layer without clumping. Even if you already have long lashes, mascara takes your lashes to another level and makes your eyes pop. We know you know this but just in case you need a refresher, always curl your lashes and add a primer before adding mascara. This will help the color to stay and be applied evenly and help with clumping.

Tip #5: Eyebrows set the tone for your look. Having nicely shaped eyebrows can frame your face nicely. Getting your eyebrows done (meaning cleaned up) can give you the confidence to conquer the world. Whether you are doing your eyebrows or having a professional handle your eyebrows, be sure to shape them to naturally fit your face. Getting your eyebrows waxed, threaded, plucked, and/or tattooed is a personal choice. Each of these options has its pros and cons. The four things you should know about having amazing eyebrows are to:

1) Know Where Your Brows Should Begin
2) Know Where Your Brows Arch Should Peak
3) Know Where Your Brows Should End
4) Never Overpluck Your Brows
5) Brush Your Brows With A Spooly Brush To Keep Eyebrows In Place

When wanting to enhance your brows there are various makeup tools you can turn to such as an eyebrow pen or pencil of your brow shade to fill in gaps and create an even fuller look. Use a clear brow gel to keep your eyebrows in place when you're ready for a night out. Depending on how you would like your eyebrows to look there are also services like tinting, microblading, micro feathering, micro shading, brow threading lift, eyebrow lamination, and powder brows. With this many options, you definitely can achieve the perfect brows.

Tip #6: Using a blush and/or bronzer is great to add a little bit of color to your cheeks. Sometimes all you need is just a little bit of blush from that glowing fresh-face look. Dry powder blush works well with just about any type of foundation you choose to use.

To achieve that sun-kissed glow effect, use a bronzer. When searching for a perfect shade bronzer we recommend using one that is about two shades darker than your complexion to start. Once you feel like you have mastered picking out the right shade of bronzer for you to use you can step away from this rule. The best areas to apply bronzer is along your cheeks, across your jawline to your chin, and blend it into your neck on both sides of your face.

Tip #7: If you are wanting to build your eye shadow collection but do not have so many we recommend that you start with neutrals, champagnes, and taupe colors. These colors work well with just about anyone's complexion and are great for layering other colors. If you are looking for a more natural look, we recommend sticking to matte colors as shimmery shades draw more light and drama. When applying eyeshadow keep colors just above your lash line and sweep across your eyelid crease.

Tip #8: We love lips that pop and there are so many ways to do that. From lipsticks, lip gloss, lip liners, lip plumpers, and lip stains you can get the shiniest, wet lip look to a neutral matte look. Before ever applying any type of lip gloss or lip product, always is sure to prep your lips. Remove any dead skin that may be on your lips and be sure to treat your lips if they are currently chapped or cracked. A great lip scrub and lip balm would help keep your lips smooth and ready for application. We always recommend applying lipstick first to the center of your lips and then spreading it from side to side. Lightly smack your lips together to spread the color evenly. If it is your desire; add a lip gloss over the lip color evenly or if you want a completely lighter, sheer look, you can skip the lipstick altogether and just apply lip gloss.

Tip #9: The final step of your makeup routine should be the use of a setting spray. A setting spray helps makeup to stay on you all day long without looking so shiny or causing greasing. It also reduces the need for reapplication. So whether you are doing a light makeup coverage or a full face of makeup, we recommend using a high-quality setting spray to keep your makeup look flawless for a long period of time. Simply spray setting spray on your face about 8-9 inches from your face and let it dry without rubbing. It will dry within seconds and you should be ready to go. To take it a step further we want to also give you this tip, use a setting spray in between each step to set applications, then use a finishing spray at the end of your complete makeup application.

Oh But Wait. This Is A List Of Our Dos And Don'ts When It Comes To Makeup Applications.

The Don'ts:

- Don't Apply Makeup On A Dirty Face
- Apply A Ton Of Product
- Use Dirty Brushes
- Apply Makeup In The Wrong Lighting
- Don't Forget Your Brows
- Sleep With Makeup

Please Do:

- Keep Your Skin Clean And Ready
- Always Apply Primer To The Face
- Blend Properly
- Choose The Right Foundation
- Find The Perfect Shade Of Lipstick
- Wash And Moisturize Your Face After Removing Makeup

Your makeup looks are up to you and can help you create your unique style identity. Use makeup to enhance your beauty. You don't always have to keep it simple and you do not always have to do bold looks. If a natural glow is what you want to achieve, you can find the right shades and products to help you achieve that. Makeup products range from traditional ingredients to some naturally made makeup products. Each has its pros and cons but you can determine what is best for you. We do recommend that you invest in good quality cosmetics as these are products that are directly applied to the skin. Being that your skin is the largest organ in your body, it is breathing in whatever you put on it. So invest in quality cosmetic items like foundation. You can mix and match drug store cosmetic products with high-end cosmetics products to achieve great results.

18

YOU MUST
SMELL LOVELY – SCENTS

Perfume Follows You; It Chases You And Lingers Behind You. It's A Reference Mark. Perfume Makes Silence Talk.

– Sonia Rykiel

You never forget a good scent. It takes you back to a special place, person and time. You never forget the person who wore that unforgettable accessory. Oh, you can and will capture a lot of hearts just because you are an IT Girl, but you'll have people telling stories about you when you wear this unforgettable accessory. You can never have too many scents in your collection. You may have a different perfume for every occasion. A daytime scent is usually light while evening scents tend to be a bit stronger with more spice. When determining what scent is best for you, we recommend wearing a scent on your skin for some time to see how it goes with your skin and sweat chemistry. Also, decide if the base note is one that you love as that is the scent that tends to linger. Top notes tend to stay on only for a few seconds but the middle note and truly the base note is what will last and be the scent you smell on your body.

These Are The Things You Should Know:

- Fragrances Will Last Longer On Skin That Is Well Moisturized Due To Oils On The Skin Trapping Fragrance Notes
- Avoid Applying Directly On Clothing
- Less Is More
- Carry A Travel Size Bottle If You Ever Need To Reapply
- The Types Of Fragrances That Last The Longest Are: Parfum, Then Eau De Parfum, Then Eau De Toilette, Then Eau De Cologne, Then Eau Fraiche.
- Always Store Fragrances In Cool Dark Places And Away From Direct Sunlight.

- You Can Layer Perfumes To Build The Perfect Signature Scent For Yourself
- Apply Your Fragrance Directly On Your Pulse Points
- When Applying On Your Wrists Do Not Rub Your Wrists Together.

Take your time in picking a fragrance that is right for you. Learn if you love ouds, musks, or fruity scents. What smells great on someone else can smell completely different on you and vice versa.

19

DOING IT FOR YOURSELF

When others see us they are always surprised by how we make things happen. We can come up with a plan and get things done. We are also able to do things for ourselves. This means we can rely on ourselves and be independent women who pay our own bills, takes care of ourselves, loves ourselves, buys ourselves the things that we want, and so on. We don't need anyone to do this for us but we like when others do. If you are currently in a position where you currently HAVE TO rely on someone to help you make it through, that is one hundred percent okay. There is such a thing as knowing what you can do for yourself verse being helpless. We are never truly independent in terms of having a team to help us to have structure in our lives. Your team (as mentioned earlier in this book) might include a personal trainer, house cleaner, etc. This doesn't mean you can't do it for yourself. It means knowing when to be able to do it for yourself and using your time and resources wisely so you can focus on the most important things to you.

If you feel like you are currently in a spot where you are not independent and are helpless, again we say no problem. It's time to get you up from the helplessness feeling and into some plan of action. As you read earlier in this book, we are all about moving strategically, setting the right goals for ourselves mentally, physically, and spiritually while staying focused and all-around elevating. Everyone will wonder how you did it. Your situation is never permanent unless you say it is. Everything and anything can change and you must be prepared for that. You may also be able to help with the direction of the change. Look at the areas in which you are depending on someone else because you have to. For example, if you are a single mother and depend on someone else to watch your kids (who is not the worst person to watch your kids but also not the best person to watch your kids) but you want to be able to have the time to watch your kids or get someone else (who is more fitted) to watch your kids, then think about what steps you would need to make and what that would look like. Now you may say things like; I have to make more money or I have to just up and quit my job, and while those things may get you the result you want right now, it may not be smart or feasible for you to do. It's also not a plan. Those are goals. Two different things. What is the plan? A starting plan if possible could be instead of working five days a week, I now work four days a week and have my child for the extra day or it can be working five days a week and spending the fourth day working from home or working on your business that will help to get you to your goal quicker. It could be instead of waking up at six in the morning you may need to wake up temporarily three times out of the week at four in the morning to do some work for yourself and go to sleep instead of ten at night at one in the morning. Doing this may help you get your child earlier or work on what you need to work on to reach your goal better. This is just a scenario of creating a plan to get you the independence you need.

As you can see when we speak about independence we speak about being able to do things for ourselves. If you can't do it for yourself, then consider hiring others to help you get things done for you when you need it the most. Independent IT Girls have a team. Having a team doesn't make you any less independent, it makes you smart and hopefully an effective boss who knows how to manage her time, money, team, and other resources. Being independent with a team is completely different from being very dependent on someone or something for your survival and being able to take care of yourself. IT Girls take pride and being and/or having the ability to be independent. If you're working to put yourself in this position, be proud. Because we all had to start somewhere and setbacks happen so how you set yourself up in this period in your life matters. Make sure to create the plan and be consistent and work on the plan to reach the goal. There may be times when you may have to adjust your aim but the target is still the same.

Please note that when we speak of independent IT Girls, we are not simply referring to single women. Independent IT Girls come in many different statuses which can be single, in a relationship, married, pregnant, a single mother, etc. …. You name it. It's not about who you are with but who you are on your own (or with a child).

20

BEING ABOUT
YOUR MONEY

We love to shop. We love to spend and we love to always look good. We love to be able to do anything we want without having the limitation of money. We love to not only splurge on ourselves but others. We love to make plans knowing that money is not a factor in those plans. We love to know that we are part of the crowd that can and not the crowd that can't. Many of us were once part of the crowd that had to say 'not now, maybe later' (and some of us on some levels are still saying this), but we love the elevation of being on the other side of the struggle. Many of this comes with having a strong money mindset.

One thing is for sure, you have to be about your money. From how you get it to how you manage it. You can make good or bad decisions that can either improve your life or financially set you back completely. Because we truly value ourselves as IT Girls, we must start making better decisions with money. We know that we must carry less debt and start to invest in ourselves. Because we have chosen to start to completely take control of our lives, we also start to take control of our financial situations and create a plan to relieve, build and create with our finances. By doing this, our net worth starts to increase as well.

Always strive to know what is going on with your money. Do not ever just hand over your money to someone to just trust them to take care of your expenses without ever looking at where your money is going. This is not called taking control. This is called not wanting to be bothered or responsible and in the end, you will always be responsible because it is your money.

While IT Girls like to splurge we also like to save and invest. Here are a few things you should be doing with your money:

- Always Pay Yourself First
- Create A Budget
- Pay Off Debt/While Investing Some Money
- Have A Savings Plan While Putting Money Away In An Emergency Fund
- Create A Retirement Plan
- Create New Avenues Of Income
- Create A Short Term And Long-Term Investment Strategy

IT Girls are smart with money and choose to expand over time with financial knowledge. We know how to generate income for ourselves without manipulating, harming, and controlling others. We are always coming up with new ways to bring in income as we know the importance of financial freedom. We know the importance of having good to excellent credit. We do not just lazily wander when it comes to money. Money is easily attracted to us and we multiply all of the money that comes into our hands (repeat this sentence to yourself and start to believe it).

Once you are in a great financial place your self-confidence skyrockets even more. If you already have ten thousand dollars, then start striving for one hundred thousand dollars. If you already have one hundred thousand dollars, start aiming for one million dollars while keeping your expenses much lower. From four figures to five figures, to six figures, then to seven, eight, and beyond, you are capable of reaching your financial goals. Growing our income is always a priority for us. Being financially stable helps us to be creative, express ourselves, give us peace of mind and expand. Educating yourself financially is important and knowing that now is the time to take your finances seriously, will help you to face any issues you currently have and overcome them.

It doesn't matter how much debt you have you can always come out of it. It doesn't matter if you have experienced bankruptcy and any other huge financial burden. What matters is the plan you create for yourself and how you overcome your hurdle because ignoring your situation is not an option if you currently are in one. We want to encourage you to stay positive and know that life changes for the better at any given moment with the intention of doing better.

For those of us who are doing well and want to do better, remember that at the end of the day we love deposits to hit our bank accounts. We love to get paid every single day. Make this a goal for yourself if you desire that. We know many opportunities will come in the form of business opportunities that can result in a positive transaction that will elevate how you view yourself, choices and IT Girl status. You never want to be the woman with the expensive bag but can't put the cost of that same bag in cash in that exact bag. You do not want to be the one who has to borrow money for non-investments (we don't mean homes or businesses). People look to you to give and it is a privilege to be on the side that can do so. Many say you can't buy love with money which is completely true but you can gain respect. Always remember a real IT Girl doesn't have to have millions to be an IT Girl but that doesn't mean she isn't about her money because she currently doesn't have that either. IT Girls have a way of making impossible situations seem easy and almost effortless while in the process of elevation and working with what they have.

21

RULES IN LOVE AND
THE GUIDELINES FOR DATING

These days, finding love has become a complicated process. Many people are scared of dating or falling in love because they are scared of how it would turn out. It can be very intimidating, especially because some level of vulnerability is involved. Not to worry, we are here to give you the rules in love and dating for an IT Girl. You could be getting it all wrong when it comes to dating because you haven't figured out how. Do you want to know how IT Girls seem to have it right when it comes to love and dating? Hang on! You're in for a good ride on that. The first thing you shouldn't forget about dating is being ready. You have to know if you're prepared to share your life with someone else and also be intimately involved in that person's life. When you finally decide that you are ready, then comes the big phase. Dating!

Whatever your case may be, your love life and dating can change positively if you follow our dating rules for an IT Girl.

Dating Rules You Should Follow

There are rules to remember when it comes to dating. They are:

1. CHOOSE A PLACE YOU ARE COMFORTABLE WITH FOR YOUR FIRST DATE: A first date is quite important because most times, it gives the people we are dating their very first impressions of us. It should be somewhere you are comfortable enough to express yourself. Go somewhere you can be you and naturally let things flow without forcing it.

2. KEEPING AN OPEN MIND: It is normal to have your specifications when it comes to dating other people, but don't let it blindfold you from seeing the beauty in others. Don't be too quick to write people off because you

think you don't share the same interests as them. You might find out the beauty in diversity too.

3. TAKE THINGS AT YOUR PACE: Don't be too quick to get into a relationship in that you don't take your time to enjoy your dating process. Take things at your own pace and be sure to decide what you want when getting into a relationship.

4. POSITIVITY: Yes! IT Girls exude positivity even when it comes to love and dating. Instead of thinking up a thousand and one ways that your date could go wrong, why don't you fill your mind with positive thoughts about your having a good time with that person?

5. DON'T REVEAL TOO MUCH YET: An IT Girl understands the importance of playing the suspense role sometimes. It makes your man eager to know more about you and will be willing to see you more often. This doesn't mean you should be secretive.

6. TRUST YOUR INTUITION: Sometimes your gut feeling might tell you things about the other person or you might sense that something is not right with your date. Your intuition might be correct. You either act upon it or you watch things unfold with time.

7. BE CHARMING: Give full attention to the other person. Show interest in the conversations. No one likes to feel left out or ignored.

8. DO NOT BE DESPERATE: It is better to be single than to rush into something you won't be happy about. Enjoy your phase of being single because it also helps you to love yourself and know yourself even more.

9. BE COMFORTABLE WITH BEING PURSUED: You do not need to force conversations to happen, initiate dates or go out of your way to show interest. Let this be the time that interest is showed to you. Be comfortable with someone going out of their way to express their

interest in you through calling, texting and just wanting to spend time with you.

10. PAY ATTENTION TO RED FLAGS: Usually we get so wrapped up in a date going well and we get so excited that what can be/should be considered a red flag is often dismissed as just a little blender. Pay attention to red flags that can reveal the type of person you are dating. Examples of some red flags would be:

- They Don't Respect Your Boundaries
- They Have A Hurtful Sense Of Humor
- They Speak Over You
- Your Values In Life Are Different
- They Want To Move Quickly In The Relationship
- How They Treat Others
- They Don't Ask Many Questions To Really Get To Know You

11. DON'T PUT OUT ON THE FIRST DATE: Of course each woman will do what they want to do but we say complete physical intimacy shouldn't happen on the first date. This is not only to hold out simply because you may not hear back from your date once they get the goods, or they may label you as this or that, but this is so you can also protect yourself and get to know the person you are dating and if you would like to share your body with this individual.

Dating Guidelines You Shouldn't Follow

1. ONLY DATE WITHIN YOUR AGE GROUP: The problem with this rule is that you limit yourself to building beautiful relationships with people you might be older or younger than. When you choose to be open with love, you'd be surprised at how you'd find true love even in the oddest

situations. Now we're not talking about dating around your grandfather's age and we're not talking about dating a minor (let's be clear).

2. KEEP TRYING TO MAKE IT WORK: Even when every sign shows that the other person is not the one for you, you want to keep trying. The loophole in this is that you keep wasting your time, energy, and resources on something that doesn't make you happy. We make things less complicated for ourselves by distancing ourselves from situations that are draining. In as much as we aren't people to give up easily, it is good that we also know when to draw the line in situations that don't work for us.

3. ONLY DATE SOMEONE WHO SHARES THE SAME INTEREST AS YOU: The truth is, it might get boring if both of you share the same interest. How about someone who has a different interest than yours? You learn about other things too and you both rarely run out of what to do. You might not know other things that you like if you kept sticking to a particular pattern. Be open to dating other people of different interests.

4. DATE ONE GUY AT A TIME: The question is why should you? You are dating so you should be having fun. A guy may end up actually being a great friend while the other is someone you might want to get to know further. Why limit your options while you are dating? If you're someone who just can't keep up and forget and mix up your dates name and feel like dating multiple individuals at one time is too much for you, then you probably should follow this rule. But if you want to have fun and just take advantage of this time of your life of dating, then we say explore and meet new people.

We recognize there are so many rules when it comes to dating but the most important thing is to be yourself. And while you may recognize that there are some things that you need to do differently when picking a partner to date (and eventually be in a relationship with), realize that your wants and needs should be expressed at one time or another if you continue to date a particular individual.

We also recognize that you have such a big heart and want to say to hell with the dating guidelines, but understand that guidelines are just that. Guidelines. They are guidelines meant to protect you in so many aspects. What feels great now or a small red flag now could be something that bothers you later, but you simply choose to ignore it because he's cute, charming, seems to be what you want, etc. Remember never to put your date on a pedestal. We mean never and we say this to protect you and your boundaries. Have fun but date wisely. Here are some things we want you to learn even if you choose to deny what we are telling you....

Tip # 1: When dating let him pay. Let him court you. Now letting him court you also means you should actually be interested in him and show that in subtle ways so both of you are not wasting your time. Learn how to let him pay for you. Always have money with you to pay for yourself but do not reach into your wallet to pay for what he can be paying for. This is the first signal of whether he can even afford to date you or even date and if he is even willing to. A gentleman would never have his lady put her hand in her purse to pay.

Tip #2: Learn to receive gifts graciously. If you know who you are and start to love yourself then you know that you deserve the best in life. If you date sees the amazingness of you and want to continue to bless you because of who you are through showering you with gifts, learn to say thank you and accept the gifts with grace. Thank you is enough. You shouldn't feel pressured to do or provide anything because your date did. The gift shouldn't be a down payment or a reason for you to do something (besides just being what it is because they want to). You do not have to expect gifts but you also shouldn't be surprised by them nor lower your boundaries because of them.

Tip #3: Support your man. If you decide to enter into relationship we say when you can, always try to show support to your man. Showing support could just be in spending time being engaged in things he likes to do, creating a stress-free environment, reminding them that you are there for them and just being emotionally available for them.

Tip #4: Lose the insecurities. When dating or in a relationship letting old and new unaddressed insecurities show itself are big red flags and can cause discomfort and unnecessary confusion and pain in a growing relationship and make your partner act in unfavorable ways due to your own insecurities. Deal with known insecurities before getting into a relationship and if an insecurity pops up while in a relationship, talk about it and be intentionally about not overthinking things. Do not compare yourself or circumstances to others and get to the root of the problem.

What To Remember When It Comes To Love

- LOVE IS BASED ON TRUST: You trust people easily when they are very honest with you. That's the same way your love will grow if you are honest with the person you love.

- LOVE IS UNCONDITIONAL: When you learn to love unconditionally, you are ready to weather the storms with your partner. You are willing to love both on the good and bad days. Standing by the one you love proves your unwavering support, and this strengthens your relationship.

- DON'T FORGET TO APPRECIATE AND COMPLIMENT YOUR PARTNER OFTEN: Appreciation is an important rule to remember when it comes to love. How do you feel knowing someone appreciates even the littlest of things you for them or they compliment you for your good qualities? It's the same way you feel good about yourself when people appreciate you, that the one you love would feel when you compliment and appreciate them, too. Your love gets stronger and your bond is tighter by the day.

- AVOID COMPARING YOUR LOVE LIFE TO OTHERS: No two relationships are the same. The way we are all different as humans is the same way we can't have the same relationships as others. There is bound to be differences and comparing your love life with that of other is quite an unhealthy way to grow your relationship. You tend to become insatiable when you start to compare your love life with others. This is because you want it to be perfect, just like you see it in the media.

- KNOW YOUR PARTNER'S LOVE LANGUAGE: Words of Affirmation, Acts of Service, Receiving Gifts, Quality Time, and Physical Touch are the five important love languages that were developed by Dr. Gary Chapman. They are important because knowing and learning not just your partner's love language but your love language helps you to build a stronger and better relationship.

- EFFECTIVE COMMUNICATION: Loving someone and not communicating effectively with that person can cause the relationship to drift apart. Communicate openly and be honest about your feelings. Some people always say they don't communicate because they are too busy to make out time to communicate. But IT Girls believe that you are never too busy for someone you love. You can always make out time out of your busy schedule to communicate with the person you love. When you communicate effectively with the one you love, your relationship blossoms because then you can figure out the problems in your relationship and you both and find ways to make it work.

The Difference Between Love And Being In Love

The degree of attraction is what differentiates love from being in love. Being in love with someone is your attraction to the person due to the idealized version of them that you have created. Loving someone is how you accept the authentic version of the person. Being in love can blindfold you from seeing the red flag in the other person. Being in love is not a bad thing because most times, it leads to loving the person. When you love someone as much as you are attracted to them, you are more focused on building and strengthening your love life with them. Even in their absence, you always want the best for them. When you're in love with someone, you crave their attention, you always want to be with them and your state of mind grossly depends on them and their attitudes towards you. Loving someone is a steady feeling that, no matter how the other person behaves or the challenges that come up, you still love the person.

Being in love is often based on emotions, which are bound to fade or change with time. Loving someone is a decision. When you choose to love someone, you are willing to go through the highs and lows with them. We hope you fall in love, choose to love the right person, and the right person you choose chooses you too.

22

HOW IT GIRLS MAKE EVERYTHING SEEM EFFORTLESS

When people see us, they assume that IT Girls always have a beautiful life; no rough moments, no hard times, just a hitch-free lifestyle. While this is not completely true, we make it easy for people to assume so with the way we can make everything seem effortless. We make everything seem so simple. It looks like we can get things done without even trying. Do you want to know how IT Girls make everything seem effortless?

Here we will give you the perfect guide on how to act effortlessly. Also, you will find out how to go about your daily lifestyle making things simple for yourself.

How IT Girls Make Everything Seem Effortless

Does this mean that as IT Girls we put in the effort to make this look effortless or do we effortlessly make things effortless? When people say we make things effortless, we simply say it took a lot of effort to make things seem effortless. To achieve this effortless outcome, we have put in so much energy, consistency, and time.

One thing you should know is that practice got us to this point. We didn't magically wake up to making things simple for ourselves. We put in a level of work and consistency to achieve this. You also need to learn to be patient because your efforts might not start yielding results as quickly as you want them to.

Not many people look effortless because it is not easy to achieve an effortless style. Some people believe that we are born with effortless styles. But that's not true. It takes effort to look effortless and that's the truth! It only looks effortless to them because they are seeing the result of all the work, consistency, and time that we have put in.

The way we act effortlessly is a reflection of our being. We go for things that we feel comfortable and confident in and this helps us stay true to ourselves.

How To Act Effortlessly

The way we handle situations tells us if we act effortlessly. We are not in control of what goes on around us, but we are in control of how we react to situations. IT Girls act effortlessly in situations. Here are a few things we do that make us act effortlessly.

- WE SEE THINGS DIFFERENTLY: We overpower the situation and this gives us the confidence we need to act calmly, even when faced with difficult situations. We approach unfavorable situations by using methods we are comfortable with. An example could be when we are to be interviewed by many people. This can be very intimidating. Even though we would want them to have a good impression of us, we don't want to be hell bent on impressing them that we forget to be our real selves. Instead, we make the situation favorable by choosing comfortable conditions out of the situation and using them to our advantage.

- WE TRY NOT TO ACT UNDER PRESSURE EVEN WHILE UNDER PRESSURE: While working under pressure, you might panic, yet you still want to give your all into what you are doing. Sadly, you only end up working yourself too much and achieving little. How about you take it calmly and act like you're not under any pressure and you have no one expecting much from you. This would go a long way in improving your productivity level.

- GAINING CONTROL OF OUR EMOTIONS: We try not to always bother ourselves, especially with things we can't change and when things don't go our way, we take it as a lesson learned and don't beat ourselves up for not getting it right.

- DON'T ONLY MAKE THINGS ABOUT YOURSELF: In our conversations with others, we make them feel valued, welcomed, and comfortable. When you show people love and care, they would also want to have you around them because you make them feel at home. This is how to act effortlessly because you put in the effort of making things about them and you effortlessly have them wanting to be around you and stare at you in admiration.

- BEING CHEERFUL: You shouldn't make life too hard for yourself by wearing a gloomy look all the time. Be happy and find fun in all that you do. This will make anything that seems like a challenge pretty much effortless for you because of how you approach it.

23

TRUSTING AND UNDERSTANDING YOUR POWER

There may have been a time in your life where it felt like things just weren't going right and you may have not had any control over anything. It may have seem like things that were happening just weren't working out in your favor and the decisions that you were making may not have seemed like the best decisions for the long run. At that point it may have caused you to doubt yourself and everything going on around you that may seem like it can't work out in your favor. So you rely on your past. Your memory tells you your old story so you don't make those same mistakes again. Well we want to tell you that was the past. You were a different person. Things happen and whatever decisions that were made then to now are learning lessons regardless of the results.

You are now in the process of becoming an IT Girl. We like to think that you already are. As of right now meaning right this moment, everything that has been done to you or because of you we ask that you let go of. Accept the current outcome and put it in your mind that you get to determine things from here. When we say accept the current outcome, we mean accept where you are and let's start building trust in ourselves right now. Your past hand is not your forever hand. That from this moment forward everything you touch turns into gold. That every decision you make is the right and best decision short term and long term. When you can let go of whatever it is that is causing you to not trust yourself you will start to stand up in your power. You will realize that every day you are making a series of decisions that are helping with your evolution and reading this book and truly exercising what has been said is definitely a way to start taking control and standing in your power. You are not powerless despite what you may think or feel. You have the ability to create anything and restructure your whole life. You can 'glow up' from here. It is in your power that you start to realize just how amazing you actually are. You must start trusting that you can and will do what is best for you no matter how challenging things may seem. Train your mind to focus only on the things you want and your end goal. It is in this time you realize where your value in yourself lies. Whatever you fear face it and let it go. Do not let the feeling of the fear actually be bigger than the fear itself. It's in this time that you learn to trust yourself, and that you allow yourself to make mistakes and still view yourself as powerful. Now is the time that you stop comparing yourself to others so that you can stand in your own power.

Being able to not only stand in your own power but understand your power is what also makes you that IT Girl. When you stand in your power, you can push yourself to your limits of being uncomfortable while sticking with your boundaries. It is in this space that you can learn to be gentle with yourself, forgive yourself, communicate with others effectively what you want and be vulnerable when necessary. You start to live in your truth and hear clearly what your spirit and/or intuition is trying to tell you. We want to tell you that after the next sentence to put the book down for five minutes and imagine right now what your world would look like if everything went right. Just imagine things going right for you all the time.

Welcome back. Those thoughts and feelings do not have to just stay and be thoughts and feelings because from this point on that is your world. Start imagining that every day with even the smallest details of things moving the way you want them to move and how you would like them to go. Declare and decree how powerful you are to yourself and start operating as if you are because YOU ARE. No more victim mentality or placing blame or finding excuses. You are changing yourself and everything around you right now. IT Girls stand in our power. We have worked on ourselves day by day to not get knocked down so easily. We know who we are and unapologetically authentically love it in our own skin. When you start to view yourself in a different light you'll realize how quickly everything will conform to you and how unstoppable you are.

24

BEING UNSHAKABLE

Unshakable – When You Are Truly At Peace And In Touch With Yourself And Nothing Anyone Says Or Does Bothers You. No Negativity Or Drama Can Touch You.

Oh to be so unshakable. When we say unshakeable with me unmesswithable. To not let anyone come in between you and well you. This is where the core of you is secure and without a doubt operates in its authenticity. When you are unmesswithable, this means you are not thrown by what others think of you, say about you, what door they think they closed on you, what they tried to stop you from achieving (or thought they did), or how they tried to take your confidence. Being unmesswithable means not being moved by emotion and focus towards negative actions meant to take your attention. IT Girls are truly unshakeable. We do not try to prove anything to anyone. We've been there and done that or never felt the need to do that at all. We focus on our strengths and we learn to let go of any form of negativity just as easily as it appeared to us. We are not attached to anything outside of us so no one can take anything from us that would shake us. The reaction that others want from us simply comes in the form of a smile, shoulder shrug and plain complete ignoring of some things.

When you are unmessablewith, people find ways to rattle your core and scare you into believing whatever they want you to believe about them, yourself, circumstances and more. The goal is typically to evoke fear within you and make you believe they have the power to control whatever aspect of your life. These types of people like to belittle you, talk over you and tease you. They only treat you like you are special in a negative way. There are times when these same individuals may find that you are too attractive, smart, or that you have whatever it is that they want to have (or take away from you) that they just find a way to get under your skin. But to be unshakeable means to no longer entertain the thoughts of these kind of individuals in our lives and to focus on ourselves.

To be unshakable you must learn to leave the drama alone and learn how to make things easy for yourself. We do not struggle with anything we do not have to. We're always praising ourselves and know that most people like to engage in cheap conversations. If you want to know what cheap conversations are, that is gossiping, too much criticism, complaining, self-imposed limitations and more. Honey, everything we love is of quality and that includes the conversations we engage in. Being unshakeable gives us the power to stay genuine to ourselves and bridge the gap of disconnect between our mind and spirit. So know that we are unshakable because we have and are working on breaking negative patterns and trust our gut feelings. Become unshakable and watch the world open up for you to get whatever it is that you want.

25

KNOWING HOW
TO GET WHAT YOU
WANT AS AN IT GIRL

K nowing what you want isn't always the problem, but knowing how to get what you want as an IT Girl takes some work. To get what you want, there are different ways to achieve that and here we have a few tips on how IT Girls like us get what they want with ease.

Ten Tips To Getting What You Want

1. KNOW WHAT YOU WANT: You can't know how to get what you want if you don't know what you want and this is why this has to be the first point. Know what you want, define your goals. Ask yourself the question, 'What do I really want?'

2. DEFINE THEIR GOALS: Women who know what they want, write their goals. This is accountability. Defining their goals sets them on the path of getting what they want

3. HAVING AN OPEN MIND: IT Girls are not afraid of failure. Hence instead of being scared of not getting something right, we believe that trying new and different things to get what we need and want.

4. BE KIND TO OTHERS: We treat people with kindness and genuine compassion. We value other people too. Even though we are resilient about getting what we want, we do not treat other people with disrespect.

5. STAY POSITIVE: You didn't hurt anybody by speaking up. The worst that could happen is that you wouldn't get what you wanted but at least you made your request known. Be positive about it. Believe that you will get what you want and be confident in this. Try to overcome your limiting beliefs. We replace negative thoughts with positive thoughts that spur us to get what we want. When your mind is filled with

negative thoughts, these thoughts hold you back and prevent you from getting what you want.

6. BE VALUABLE: People of value have higher chances of getting what they want. This is how IT Girls can get what they want effortlessly. We are valuable people and we know this and use it to our advantage. Make yourself valuable to people around you from today and see how easy things will get for you.

7. RESILIENCE: Finally, IT Girls are not quitters. Once we set our minds towards achieving something, we go for it. This is how resilient you should be in getting what you want.

8. NOT ALWAYS BOTHERED ABOUT WHAT PEOPLE THINK: Caring about what people would think of, is a silent dream killer. It makes you scared of going for what you want because you are unsure of how people would react. IT Girls know who they are and

9. EMBRACE UNCERTAINTY: We embrace the uncertainty that things might not go our way but we are able to move past the fear of this uncertainty and still go for what we want because we know in the end we will get want if not better.

10. MAXIMIZE YOUR STRENGTHS: We all have our strengths and weaknesses but your weaknesses should not define you. Learning to maximize your strength is a powerful tip for knowing how to get what you want. Your confidence level rises when you know your strengths and use them to your advantage.

IT Girls are among women who know how to get what they want. We use different skills which have been mentioned already to achieve this. However, there is one vital method that most people don't know of. It is the use of our feminine energy. We know when to use our feminine energy to our advantage. Safe to say, we saved the best point for the last!

26

HOW TO EXUDE POSITIVITY

There is just something about us IT Girls that makes many people want to be like us. To most people, IT Girls are simply fashionable and attractive ladies. However, this is only a surface view of the many qualities of IT Girls. IT Girls are ladies whose qualities are beyond definable. We have an alluring personality that makes us simply irresistible.

You might wonder why we have such contagious energy that is admirable, and you are just at the right place to discover the secret behind all the energy. Positivity!

IT Girls exude positivity all the time. When you are positive about things, people see you as a nice and easy-going person. Exuding positivity involves being optimistic in many situations we find ourselves in.

How To Exude Positivity – Our Tips

We have discussed in detail below, actionable tips on how to exude positivity.

1. SMILE: Yes! You read this right. Smile. We used this as the first point because we want you to practice this while reading the rest of this section. Imagine you needed to ask for help from someone and you met two random people; one person was smiling and the other person was expressionless. Whom would you be more comfortable asking your question? Unless you don't like cheerful people, we're sure you would approach that person who is full of smiles. That's the same thing about IT Girls. We smile often and this puts people at ease with us. It is what creates this admiration for us and makes us prettier. We recommend that you should smile and laugh often.

2. CONSTANT SELF-DEVELOPMENT: As IT Girls, we are always working towards becoming better versions of ourselves, and therefore we pay

so much attention to self-development. Self-development involves learning new things and developing good habits. It also involves taking care of ourselves and taking breaks when necessary to stay happy. The confidence we get from self-development helps us stay positive because we know we are making progress, no matter how small it is. Healthy habits like surrounding yourself with positive minds and starting your mornings with positivity are very helpful. Early mornings are usually the best times to plan your day. Having a productive morning helps us remain positive for the rest of the day. Having people with unique vibes around you is also a way of building a positive mindset. Just like you are reading about how IT Girls exude positivity, you are feeding your mind with positivity too, and this is also a form of self-development.

3. ALWAYS SPEAK AND FEEL GOOD ABOUT YOURSELF: You can't radiate positivity if you don't think or speak well of yourself. When you believe in yourself and you make positive affirmations about yourself, it sets you on the path of positivity. Live a little and don't be too hard on yourself when things go wrong. IT Girls always try to see things from the better side and we worry less about things that we can't change or fix. Instead, we put in the effort to make things work. You should have a level of confidence in yourself that makes you happy. So here's the thing: whenever that crazy negative thought about you're not being good enough comes knocking, remind yourself of why you should stay positive and shut the negative thought by replacing it with a positive mindset. Make a list of good things about you and say them to yourself. The aim is to make you stay grateful and appreciative of what you have, no matter how little.

4. MAKING OTHER PEOPLE FEEL BETTER: How do you feel when you notice that someone is happy because of what you did for them, said

to them, or gave them? There is this feeling of happiness that comes with knowing you made someone smile. IT Girls are not selfish people because we think about others and show love and affection to people. We are empathic and sensitive to other people's feelings. This genuine act of kindness and affection that we display lightens our moods and spurs positivity in us. Treating people nicely, complimenting them, and appreciating their worth help you build healthier relationships with them.

5. SEEING THE BEST IN SITUATIONS: IT Girls might be portrayed as always having perfect lives, but we also face different challenges from time to time. We experience setbacks, failures, and losses sometimes, but positivity helps us get through it all. Not expecting the worst outcome in every situation, and not being deterred by the situation of things, helps us remain positive. When you learn to see the best in situations, just like other IT Girls do, you won't be afraid of mistakes because you are filling your minds with the best possible outcome of things. This is also what helps you to keep pushing, regardless. Positivity does not come by complaining all the time. You should stop beating yourself up when things don't go your way. When you learn to approach situations with an open mind, you experience happiness, even in the face of challenges. Having a positive attitude enables us to have better relationships with others. It makes us not to fear challenges and above all; it places us in a desirable position.

Positivity is a trait that comes from within. The way we interact with the world gives people the reflection of who we truly are. A positive mind is attractive and if you truly want to become as irresistible as IT Girls, then you should learn to stop expecting the worst outcome in every situation. Drowning in negativity helps no one, but positivity also takes effort that is worth all your efforts. To exude positivity, pay attention to how you react to situations, be self-aware, and consciously practice positivity every time. With time, you'll get used to this and you'll see that it's such a beautiful way to live.

Now you know why IT Girls have seemingly perfect lives!

27

BEING UNFORGETTABLE

Be Easy To Love, Hard To Break, And Impossible To Forget.

Well let's face it, with everything we've discussed in the last few chapters how could you even think that you would be someone that others do not think twice about? Whether it's their first and only time meeting you or repeatedly having several encounters with you, there is no way with everything we discussed you could easily be forgotten. To easily be remembered for your most positive traits and even your beauty, sense of style, and personality it's truly because you don't have to try to be anything you are not. You are yourself and are not out here living for others. You give because you want to, you're a pleasure to be around, you have an attractive personality and you're not one who is into mind games. You are everything they have heard about you that is positive and they want to see it for themselves. You're unforgettable because you are a genuine moment. You're unforgettable because you're inspiring. Because you are choosing to stick to the version of you that you see yourself being, you become that in everyone's eyes.

IT Girls are unforgettable because we have our own sense of style, our own sense of beauty, ideas, opinions, ambitions, and ultimately our own sense of self. We're unforgettable because we are sexy in our most feminine form and comfortable in our skin and we are unapologetic about who we are. We are women who love others as they are and make them feel so comfortable in their skin while inspiring them that we become unforgettable to them.

We often have a great reputation or currently actively building a great reputation when most people speak about us from how we make them feel. There are a few signature aspects that we are always remembered for as well. This can be our communication skills, cooking skills, the way we dress, smell, and the absence of always having a special moment or overall great experience with us.

To be unforgettable you should ask yourself what do you want to be remembered for? What do you want others to always say about you? What do you want to be able to always say about you? Once you know the answer to these questions, then take the answer and work on it until it is natural for you. Be sure to do it (whatever you came up with) with such ease and with a great attitude that you do not even realize that you have to work on it (whatever it is that you were working on) anymore, because it just comes to you so effortlessly while making others say wow.

28

HELPING OTHERS

Now we know we have talked so much about focusing on yourself and the way you view yourself. We have dissected working from the inside out in the becoming of an IT Girl that we must also acknowledge what we do for others. While we naturally inspire and influence others through our evolution of ourselves we also find ways to help others.

We know how good it is to help others and can even relate at times to the ones in need of help. Helping others provides us a sense of happiness, and a way to extend love. When helping others we open up ourselves more to connection, love, peace, and joy. We choose to help others not only because of what it does for us but what it does for the receiver as well. We love being great givers and the more we practice doing that the more we become greater and greater at it.

Knowing that you can create a change in someone else's life brings about satisfaction. The more you give the more you want to give. Whether that is time, money, or any sort of resources you'll start to realize the change that you can provide within someone's life is far more important than doing nothing and just keeping to yourself.

Now you may be wondering whom should you help. Do you help those who do not believe in you? Do you help those who treat you badly? Do you help those who can't help you when you are in need? Like who is it do you help? In general, we like to say to use discretion and help those who need help. Whether you view them as having more than you or not or if they even treated you badly in the past or not. We're not saying be friends with anyone or continue communication, but if you can and it doesn't put you or anyone close to you in harm's way, we suggest you to consider it. We are not mean girls, we are IT Girls. This means we do not think and act like everyone else. We always rise above certain mental limited conditions. Truly tit for tat is not our style. So when we give we change lives for others as well as for ourselves.

29

LIVING YOUR LIFE ON YOUR TERMS

The thing about IT Girls is that we mainly live life on our terms. We create our own rules for our own life. We see how we want our lives to go and decide that that is the direction that we will take. We can't tell you what exactly it means to live life on your terms because well you create the terms and what that means to you. You may have limited terms that you live by or a term-free life and that could apply to many different aspects of your life such as work, family, relationships, money, travel, health, etc.

Living your life on your terms for us means living in ways that you want to live. Not how your parents, friends, spouse, society, or anyone else says you need to live it to have this or that. But living in a way that you won't regret that you didn't prioritize what is important to you. To start living life on your terms, figure out what is important to you. What do you believe matters to you right now? Yes, what matters to you right now (to your heart and spirit) can and probably will change, but it will lead you to what will matter in the next phase of your life. Once you know that, you want to start honoring what matters to you and making the inner changes within yourself to live in a way where what is important to you makes you happy and is the priority.

When you decide that you want to be the IT Girl living life on her terms, you now have to let go of the individuals in your life that will not allow you to do so. Those individuals are those who tell you how you 'should be' living and what you 'should be' doing. Those individuals constantly point out your flaws and if you are not careful, they do it enough to where you have to build yourself back up from repeatedly being told who you are not and the limitations of your life. Listening to these individuals can warp the way you view yourself and your inner conversations. You will start to believe that that is the way to actually live life and you'll even think that you are living life on their terms, but you can never fully live life on their terms because it will never be good enough. Many of them aren't even living the life they want on their own terms so be careful with whom you listen to and surround yourself with individuals who encourage you to live a happy healthy life as yourself on your terms. Your life should be a life that you define. Only you can do it. Only you know your core values and beliefs and can set clear goals that hold you accountable for living this kind of life and by doing this you can start to take responsibility for your happiness. Because happiness is from within, you can decide to be happy with the decisions you are making from this point on. Living life on our terms allows us to stay focused on ourselves. This means we mind our business. We are not here, there, and everywhere with what others are doing and saying. We don't compare ourselves to others and see if the grass is greener over there. The grass is greener wherever we are. It's always better where we are because we are the ones building what we want for ourselves and living it as we want to live. We are our blueprint. We can be inspired by others but the journey is always our own. So move into the space of running forward towards living life on your terms and what that looks like. Remove the self-doubt and start cultivating the sense that you will get what you want and live how you want no matter what. This is your life. In the same way, you can't control another person's life without their permission, no one can control yours. So open yourself up to challenges and opportunities but don't give up on living on your terms because of how things seem to be or your past. You've got this.

30

CHANGING YOUR LIFE
IN SIX MONTHS

We have covered so much and given so many steps and tips for actual application. Everything we have discussed is not only about inner work but also about creating your brand. Whether you realized this or not you are your walking advertisement of who you are and what you are about and everything that you do from the inside out will show this. Doesn't matter if it's in real life or on social media. You should truly understand that by now everything you are doing, you are doing for yourself while creating the image of your IT Girl self. This is the time that things will now change. It all depends on what you do once you finish reading this book. Will you just have read the book or actually implement what we have tried to convey to you? Will you build the discipline to work on yourself? We want this to be the time that you change your life. We know that you are on your journey to being an IT Girl and know that along your journey your whole life is about to change. Not just because of the changes you are about to make but for the unexpected wonderful thoughts and events that will naturally matriculate due to you now stepping into your power and now becoming. We believe you can truly change your life in the next six months for the better and become the amazing IT Girl you want to be by just applying the things we covered in this book. Now, will it take six months? We do not know because it all depends on your consistency and seriousness to the inner and outer work you are willing to put in. We know that you can see positive changes much sooner than that but we believe six months is a great benchmark for you to be able to assess your progression in how you feel and view yourself. We suggest looking back in this book as well as keeping a daily journal of the changes you have made and the result to them. We want to remind you to not neglect the inner work and only focus on the outer work as they go hand in hand. This is the time to build up your self-confidence and decide the woman you will be right now. We have said several times within this book that you are already an IT Girl because we wanted to speak that into you. Once you are done with this book, take the time to complete the following exercises and assess where you are and what about you is about to change.

Here Are The Following Exercises To Complete:

- Write Down How You Currently View Yourself
- Write Out Who You Believe You Are
- Write Down Who You Want To Be
- Ask Yourself What Does 'Glowing Up' Look Like For You?
- Write Down What Part Of Yourself And Your Life Feels Like It Is Missing Something
- Ask Yourself How Can You Authentically Be An IT Girl?
- Ask Yourself What Is The Plan To Elevate Your Current Circumstances?
- Ask Yourself How Can You Increase Your Self-Confidence, Influence, Femininity, And More?
- Ask Yourself How Do You Currently Deal With Situations And What About How You Currently Deal With Situations Would You Like To Change?
- Ask Yourself What Is Your Personal Style?
- Ask Yourself How Will You Start Caring For Your Hair, Skin, Clothes, And More?
- Ask Yourself How Will Your Financial Life Change In The Next Six Months?
- Ask Yourself What Will You Stop Worrying About And Allow For It To Play Out Effortlessly?
- Ask Yourself What Are You Choosing To Take Control Of?
- Ask Yourself What Is Important To You?
- Ask Yourself What Goals Do You Have For Yourself?
- Ask Yourself What Will You Focus On In The Next Six Months?
- Ask Yourself When Will You Start Believing That You Are An IT Girl?

So now that you have been equipped with the actual knowledge of who and what an IT Girl is from inside and out, it is time to realize that you can be whomever you wish, just be authentically you and never allow someone to label you what you know you are not. Start making changes right now and be consistent with your daily efforts. Step into the role of being an IT Girl. Let no one take you away from the IT Girl world. Do not let what others say about you allow you to lose focus or allow your past to jeopardize what you can have right now. You deserve the best. You deserve quality and you deserve to steer the course and make the next six months completely about you. These months are your transformational months. Transform in the mind and transform in your body and how you view your world. Then let everything around you transform because of what you command for yourself. You'll find that in such a short amount of time, you'll fall so in love with yourself in the most incredible way that others can't help to feel the same way about you as well.

Remember That Girl You Are IT.
Always Have Been
And Always Will Be.

We would like to take this time to say we love you and thank you for the incredible outpouring of love towards our book. We have so much more to share and so much more to come. We ask that you continue to show support by referring another woman (whom you know should have this information) to purchase the book and shine like the IT Girl that you know they are. If you would like to be alerted on our other new exclusive products first, sign up at www.itgirlluxury.com.

Love you IT Girls! www.itgirlluxury.com

Made in the USA
Monee, IL
11 April 2023

31175042R00103